Engaging Philosophy

A Brief Introduction

Engaging Philosophy

A Brief Introduction

Mitchell S. Green

Hackett Publishing Company, Inc.
Indianapolis/Cambridge

In a republican nation, whose
citizens are to be led by reason
and persuasion and not by force,
the art of reasoning becomes of
the first importance.

— *Thomas Jefferson*

Printed in the United States of America

06 07 08 09 1 2 3 4 5 6 7

For further information, please address
Hackett Publishing Company, Inc.
P.O. Box 44937
Indianapolis, IN 46244-0937

www.hackettpublishing.com

Cover photograph: comstock.com

Cover design by Brian Rak and Abigail Coyle
Interior design by Elizabeth Wilson
Composition by Scribe
Printed at Edwards Brothers, Inc.

Library of Congress Cataloging-in-Publication Data

Green, Mitchell S.
Engaging philosophy: a brief introduction / Mitchell S. Green.
p. cm.
Includes bibliographical references and index.
ISBN 0-87220-797-8 (cloth : alk. paper) — ISBN 0-87220-796-X (pbk. : alk. paper)
1. Philosophy—Introductions. I. Title.
BD21.G74 2006
100—dc22

2005025433

The paper used in this publication meets the minimum requirements of American National Standard for Information Sciences—Permanence of Paper for Printed Library Materials, ANSI Z39.48–1984.

∞

Contents

For my parents,
Isabel and Burton Green,
who never doubted me.

Preface

This book grows out of nearly twenty years of teaching philosophy, first as a graduate student at Oxford University and the University of Pittsburgh, and then on the faculty of the University of Virginia. Over the years I've felt torn between exposing students primarily to historical works, warts and all, and offering them textbook versions of philosophy that tend to present the field as if it consisted of so many specimens under glass. Neither approach is fully satisfactory: The former risks putting off all but the most intrepid, while the latter offers an image of philosophy as sealed off from everyday concerns. In response to this tension, I have generally asked students to read primary sources while, in my lectures, doing my best to bring to life the philosophers they were reading by making clear how much these philosophers' interests engage with our own. With the benefit of years of constructive input from my students, friends, and colleagues, this book is an attempt to refine, clarify, and elaborate those lectures into a format that is self-contained but also suitable to be read in conjunction with primary sources.

This book would not have been possible without input from many of the thousands of students it has been my privilege to teach over the years. Nor could I have written it without the love and moral support of my wife Lori, or the love, moral support, and comic relief of my children, Noah and Sofia. My research assistant Ana Balan offered detailed and insightful criticism on many points, and helped to compile the index. My students Ayca Boylu, Malayna Ford, and Patrick Toner each read an earlier draft of the manuscript and offered excellent suggestions for improvement. So did Brian Cohen and Lisa Marshall, who give me confidence that this book will be of interest to the general adult reader. In addition, my colleague John Marshall has offered me extensive comments on an earlier draft, and saved me from at least one blunder. My editor at Hackett Publishing Company, Brian Rak, has judiciously guided and encouraged this project. I am also grateful for the care and patience given this book by my project editor at Hackett Publishing Company, Liz Wilson, and my copyeditor, Jennifer Albert. Finally, I am indebted to Nuel Belnap, Joe Camp, and Richard Gale. They taught me how to teach.

1. Introduction

In many areas of inquiry, introductions provide fundamental information. That, however, is not the only, and perhaps not the most effective way of making an introduction to philosophy. Instead, to convey the excitement and importance of the field I find it most effective to elicit a skill. In fact, not many people are truly new to philosophy; if you've ever tried to reason systematically about issues pertinent to important real-life decisions that are not settled by scientific or mathematical proof, you've already been using this skill. As a result, one way of "introducing" philosophy is to remind readers of something they've been doing for some time.

Suppose that you've been to see a movie with friends and head for coffee afterward. One friend remarks, "I didn't like that movie much. The main character was a self-centered jerk, and he ended up not getting in trouble for what he did." Another replies, "I can't believe you're saying this! That character Devlin was just looking out for himself like any reasonable person does, and after all in the real world it's not as if when you do something wrong you always get punished." You chime in, tentatively, "Well, is doing right or wrong just a matter of looking out for Number One? And anyway, even if we don't get punished for wrongdoing in this life we might get punished in some other life?" Your two friends look at you with a mixture of scorn and pity, one of them saying, "That's just old Sunday School claptrap. You still believe that? Your priest seems to have ignored all the trouble there is in the world out there, and if he hadn't ignored it he would have stopped believing in his God long ago. And if there's no God there's no morality either. Look out for Numero Uno is what I say. Devlin's got it going on." The conversation goes until closing time.

You and your friends have been engaging philosophy, maybe without knowing it. Or better: You've been exchanging opinions on philosophical issues, and while you may never have reflected on some of those opinions before, other opinions of yours might have been the subject of sustained reflection on your part. When you begin to consider these opinions not as going without saying but rather as requiring some support, when you begin to see that other opinions might be held on the same issues without making those who hold them necessarily unreasonable, when you consequently strive to find reasons in support of one of these opinions as against another—that's when you begin to exercise the skill that is philosophy. The more adept you become at this skill, the more philosophical you are. In fact, you can have a philosophical mind without knowing much about which famous philosopher held what theory at what time. What makes famous philosophers famous is their stunning exercise of philosophical skill; but just as you can be a superb chess player without studying the techniques of the masters of the past, you can develop philosophical skill without consulting the history of the field.

You probably already have opinions about many important and controversial issues, and I've just told you that you can study philosophy without being required to absorb lots of information. What, then, is the good of self-consciously and painstakingly engaging philosophy as I've just characterized it? Well, here are three ways in which engaging philosophy can be worthwhile.

First of all, *opinions aren't knowledge.* Until you can see how to find reasons on behalf of your opinions, even heartfelt opinions that you've cherished for much of your life, why are you confident that they're anything more than prejudice? Further, even if such opinions are not prejudices in the sense of being held out of contempt or spite, they will still not be ones that you can back up with reasons. And yet, what a pity if your life is guided by opinions that you cannot support with reasons. The philosopher Immanuel Kant once referred to this as "dogmatic slumber."

Another reason for striving to go beyond opinion has to do with the *suppleness of mind* you can develop in the process. By becoming alive to the controversial nature of views that guide some of our most momentous decisions, you develop an alertness to the complexity and depth of questions central to human life. This alertness will better enable you to see both sides of a controversial issue, thereby facilitating your understanding of others who hold positions opposed to your own. You'll probably continue to disagree with such people, but rather than finding them obtuse or perverse, now you will be able to understand where they are coming from. Such an understanding may help you to become more empathetic, thereby fostering communication with people whose attitudes are quite different from your own. It can also encourage modesty as you come to see that your own position might reasonably be doubted.

A third reason for cultivating philosophical skill is *practical:* Philosophers are sometimes described as professional arguers, and that's no accident. Philosophical skill comprises an ability to argue on behalf of a controversial position, and you are likely to have many opportunities to do so in the future in addition to those that have already come your way. You may someday find yourself attempting to convince your colleagues where your business should invest; how to adjudicate a patient's right to life against limited healthcare resources; or why a geographical area or endangered species needs to be protected against development. Or you may be faced with hard decisions about how to educate your children or whether a loss in job satisfaction is worth a gain in income. In all these cases and many others, not only is it of immense value to be able to convince others of a controversial opinion, but it is also of great value to be able to answer your own question, prodding you awake in the small hours, "Am I doing the right thing?" Philosophy can help you develop the skills to answer questions like this reflectively and deliberately.

When I say, "develop the skills to answer questions," I do not mean that engaging philosophy, much less reading this book, will provide you definitive answers to these questions. Even the most sophisticated philosophical positions can be vulnerable to criticism in one way or another. Nonetheless, a popular misconception about philosophy is that it offers answers to the big questions.[1] Such answers can help to banish those late-night doubts I mentioned a moment ago, and they make it easier to ignore people with positions different from yours. Bookstores make handsome profits selling books that cater to our desire for mental comfort. However, books peddling answers to the so-called big questions belong in the self-help or inspirational sections rather than the philosophy section. Responsible philosophers are painfully aware of the controversial nature of their subject matter, and they try to be forthcoming about it. In fact, given our description of philosophy as a skill rather than a body of information, someone offering answers to the big questions should be looked on with no less suspicion than someone offering to teach you piano by letting you watch him play. Instead, engaging philosophy can help you to find the strongest evidence you can for answers to questions that each of us must face at one time or another in our lives. Better to face these questions with reasons rather

[1] A colleague of mine was on an airplane chatting with another passenger. When this new acquaintance found out that he was a philosophy professor he asked, "Well, what are some of your sayings?"

than habit or dogma, even if in the end those reasons might still be vulnerable to some doubt.

Some people, upon finding out that philosophy tends not to offer definitive answers to the big questions, overreact and conclude that philosophy is nothing but endless wrangling. After all, one might point out, many of these questions have been with us at least since Socrates, Plato, and Aristotle practiced their art 2,300 years ago. Shouldn't we have figured it all out by now? Two remarks are relevant to this impatient pessimism. First of all, part of what makes a question philosophical is that people asking it don't yet know how to settle it with experiments or mathematical proof. Once they do, however, the question tends to cease being philosophical. For instance, psychology was a branch of philosophy until researchers began to see how to test certain claims about the workings of the mind, at which point psychology began to develop as a field of its own. As a result, however, by the time a question that was once philosophical became an issue for psychology, the ability to answer it experimentally no longer looked like a philosophical advance. For this reason, philosophy can appear destitute to the untrained eye because it can't be bothered to settle down with its children. The astute observer, however, sees that philosophy's assets include not only many foundations for contemporary departments of knowledge but also freedom of movement itself.

Second, it is true that many questions have remained philosophical questions for over two millennia. Among these are questions about morality, free will, knowledge, and the self. However, we know a great deal more than ever before about the forms that these questions can take and the range of admissible answers to them. In fact, the last fifty years have seen an explosion of such knowledge as witnessed by the proliferation of journals and monographs on these and other ancient questions. In addition, though, two millennia or so is really just chump change relative to the history of our species; it's even a small fraction of the history of civilization. For this reason, those who throw up their hands in frustration at the fact that philosophers still debate questions of, say, ethics, just as Socrates did, are being impetuous: After all, they're among the hardest questions a thinking person can ask.

I have written this book in the hope of introducing the absolute newcomer to philosophy—although as I explained above in many cases I may be reminding you of what you've already been doing. I hope this book is also of use to those who studied philosophy in the past and would like to be refreshed. I have striven to presuppose no technical or other background knowledge in the reader other than general common sense and a desire to think carefully and critically. When I do use jargon, I define it as best I can, and those definitions appear again in the Glossary. Also I hope, by means of this introductory book, to give you a sense of the field and the skills it involves, but I do not aim to provide a comprehensive overview of the field or any of the topics it contains. That is for more advanced reading or course work. If this book is successful, however, it will provoke some readers to pursue topics that interest them in greater depth. To that end, at the close of each chapter other than this one I offer suggestions for further reading as well as a brief list of movies pertinent to the topic of that chapter. You may be surprised at how many movies engage, either self-consciously or implicitly, with philosophical issues, and watching these movies in light of what you've read is a good way not only to enhance your philosophical understanding but also to deepen your appreciation of the art form of film.

Each chapter other than this one also ends with a set of study questions. I hope that you use these questions not only to test your understanding of the material covered in the chapter just completed but also to challenge yourself to develop your own ideas in response to what I have written. One useful approach is to write out answers to as many of these questions as you can. Another is to use these questions as a basis for discussion with others who may be reading the book or who are interested in the topics it addresses. In keeping with my idea that philosophy is as much an exercise of skill as it is a body of knowledge, one way to start developing your skills is to answer these study questions. You may be surprised by how satisfying it is to engage with these questions actively, especially in the company of others, rather than passively.

This book is a "topical" introduction, meaning that we will be engaging philosophy through a number of questions that lie at the field's core. In the course of this engagement we will consider a variety of potential answers to each of the questions that we raise. I hope to make the case that each of these questions is one that any person from any walk of life or cultural milieu can raise; likewise anyone's answers can be challenged or improved upon by anyone else. This means that we might discuss a question that one philosopher of ancient Greece, another from the European Renaissance, and a third from twentieth-century India all tried to answer, and we can assess the cogency of all three answers. If none of these answers is persuasive, we might formulate our own. This topical approach differs in emphasis, though not entirely in content, from a historical approach. The historical approach to philosophy typically marches through a stretch of time explaining which philosophers or schools held what views and how one position influenced another subsequent to it. Our topical approach will pay attention to the views of historically significant philosophers and their schools of thought, but only insofar as their positions offer answers to the questions that we will be pursuing.

Another feature of the topical approach that recommends it for an introductory book is that it enables us to see philosophy as an ongoing enterprise, as a work in progress rather than a relic under a display case. Today professional philosophers are actively engaged with questions in ethics, religion, politics, the arts, science, and many other fields. Some professional philosophers study the views of the great figures of the past, and this is a fascinating, technically demanding, and painstaking enterprise. However, many others see the history of the field as a profound source of inspiration, but they nonetheless focus on current, vexing problems and their solution. This latter point of view sits well with our topical approach, where what matters is not who (Plato, Gandhi, your great aunt, etc.) said what about the problem at hand, but whether what they said is a good answer.

Chapter 2 covers some fundamental concepts in the field of logic. In it we shall give a brief overview of the absolutely essential concept of an argument, and we shall learn some basic techniques for distinguishing compelling arguments from those that are not compelling—the so-called fallacies. In addition, the chapter discusses not only techniques for decision making but also some errors to which this process is prone. In Chapter 3 we will investigate whether it is possible to find any rational basis for belief in God. We will also consider whether disbelief in God can be rationally justified. Important in this area, which is known as the philosophy of religion, is the topic of evil, and our discussion of evil will serve as a transition into Chapter 4, which is concerned with the source of morality: Do moral systems have their bases in social conventions, individual rights, divine decree, subjective opinion, rationality, or something else?

Chapters 5, 6, and 7 are concerned with metaphysics. In Chapter 5 we will consider what a mind is, and whether it is possible to make sense of some of the peculiar properties of minds in an otherwise apparently mindless world. In Chapter 6 we take up the challenge of understanding how the will might be free in a world that seems to be entirely governed by causes. Is my being a free agent in tension with the fact that my actions seem to have their source in events outside me? If so, then given that our praise and blame of one another depends on the assumption of freedom, does this tension show that morality is an illusion? Finally, in Chapter 7 we will investigate the difference between hunks of matter and persons, and try to find out in what that difference consists. Is being a person simply a matter of being a *Homo sapiens,* or does the category of a person somehow have a different source than biology?

Finally, I have written each chapter with the aim of making it as self-contained as possible. This means that if you are more interested in the mind than in ethics, for instance, you don't have to read Chapter 4 before reading Chapter 5. However, all chapters presuppose that you know what a good argument is, what a fallacy is, and the difference between soundness and validity. These issues are covered in Chapter 2, on reasoning. Thus, Chapters 3 through 7 presuppose Chapter 2, but none of Chapters 3 through 7 presuppose any of the others. Let's get started, then, with the study of reasoning.

2. Reasoning: Truth and Prudence

In the introductory chapter I told you that philosophy raises and tries to answer central questions that apparently cannot be settled by scientific inquiry. Some of these questions concern what is in fact the case: Is the will free? Is the mind distinct from the body? Is there a God? These are just three of the many questions of this sort, and they are among those that we'll be considering in later chapters. By contrast, some questions concern what we should do: How shall I behave in order to live virtuously? How shall a just society organize itself? While the what-is-the-case questions inquire into how things are, what-to-do questions inquire into how we should behave. Answers to the former try to show certain beliefs are rational to hold. Some, but not all, of the suggested answers to the latter try to establish certain actions as being reasonable.

Theoretical rationality concerns the ways in which one can support a proposition by showing it is true or likely to be true. It is, accordingly, theoretically rational to believe a proposition just in case one has adequate evidence in its favor. By providing evidence for the carcinogenic properties of nicotine we attempt to show that it is theoretically rational to believe that nicotine causes cancer. By providing evidence for the existence of God we try to show that belief in God is theoretically rational.

By contrast, *practical rationality* concerns how actions and ensembles of actions are reasonable in light of such considerations as an agent's desires and expectations. Advising a friend to eat healthily counsels him to do something that will serve his best interests, at least in the long run. In comparison to a diet of junk food, a healthy diet, you might point out, will increase his chances of living longer, of being in better health, and of keeping off excess weight. Similarly, to convince someone that honesty is the best policy you do well to show her that telling the truth is in her best interests. After all, if she is a liar she runs a risk of developing a reputation for being a liar, with the result that no one will take her word seriously in the future. Similarly, as we'll see in the next chapter, one argument for belief in God does not try to offer evidence of God's existence (doing so would make belief in

God theoretically rational), but rather tries to show that it is practically rational to believe in God. Traditionally, logic studies theoretical rationality, while decision theory studies practical rationality. It will be useful for later topics in this book for us to consider both theoretical and practical rationality.

Grounds for Belief

In discussing reasons for the existence of a divine being, for a position about abortion, for intervention in the affairs of foreign countries, or for the physical basis of consciousness, one often hears the phrase "grounds for belief." Beware: This notion of "grounds" hides an ambiguity. On the one hand a person discussing grounds for belief might have in mind a historical or psychological account of the origin of that belief. Thus if I am a sexist who believes, for instance, that a woman's place is in the home, the ground of that belief might be that I was brought up to believe this. This would be reflected in the fact that if someone asked me why I believe this, I might reply with something like, "I was brought up to think this way." Similarly, the ground of my belief in a divine being might be that I was raised in a devout household. Note, however, that these kinds of "ground" for belief aren't going to justify anyone else in thinking in a way similar to mine; in fact, if I reflect on the basis of my sexism I might well find good reason to doubt whether that view about women is a *reasonable* or in some other way appropriate thing to hold. Merely remembering where my belief came from is not going to help me decide whether it's a reasonable one.

The fact that we can cite the cause or history of a belief is not enough to show that the belief is a rational or appropriate thing to hold. How *would* we show this? One way would be to present a body of evidence that would adequately support the belief in question. That is, we could support the belief by showing it to be theoretically rational. Belief that the Sun is the center of the solar system, that disease is spread by such things as bacteria and viruses, or that continental drift is caused by shifting of the Earth's plates, is rational—if it is—by virtue of theoretical rationality. We believe one of these things because we have adequate evidence in its favor.

Yet theoretical rationality is not the only possible vindication of a belief. In addition to theoretical rationality, one can be rational in holding a belief if for some reason holding it is sufficiently expedient. I'm quite confident that smoking tends to cause lung cancer. Suppose, however, that an executive of a large tobacco concern approaches me and offers to pay me an exorbitant sum if I take a pill, which he is holding in his hand and which will affect my brain in such a way that I will become convinced that smoking does *not* cause lung cancer. Most of the rest of my beliefs will remain intact; the pill will just make the minimal changes required for me consistently to believe that smoking doesn't pose a health threat. The amount the executive offers is so enticing that I agree to take the pill. After all, if I had that amount of money, I could endow a large source of fellowships for underprivileged students to attend college, to say nothing of fixing the leak in my roof! Also, before taking the pill I am assured that if I am not a smoker, taking the pill won't make me one. So in light of all these reasons I take the pill and, lo and behold, in a week's time I am sure that tobacco is no carcinogen. Now I can live comfortably and help others in need. The belief that the pill has brought about in me is not theoretically rational—we know that the evidence strongly supports the carcinogen theory, and the pill doesn't give me any evidence to the contrary. My believing that tobacco is no carcinogen is nevertheless practically rational: It's in my best interests to believe that smoking is no health threat.

In the area of belief, then, we can distinguish between causal or historical bases or grounds that do not, just by themselves, show a belief to be rational or in some other way appropriate, and other kinds of ground that do. Within the latter category, we can then distinguish between grounds that show a belief to be theoretically rational and grounds that show it to be practically rational. Yet another "ground" for a belief might come in the form of a *moral* injunction. Perhaps there are certain beliefs that we are morally obliged to hold. For instance, imagine that a close friend has been accused of a crime. Lots of her other friends seem to be deserting her, and you feel that she has no one to turn to but you. You might on this basis believe that she is innocent of the crime in question, avowing this belief both to her and to her accusers. Someone might challenge you: "Look, there's a fair bit of evidence implicating her in this crime. Why do you persist in maintaining her innocence?" In response you point out that you owe it to your friend to stand behind her; this is what friends do. If you do answer this way, then you are justifying your belief not on causal or historical grounds, not on grounds of either theoretical or practical rationality, but instead on moral grounds. Those moral grounds might be quite compelling; you may be doing the right thing in holding the view you do. You may well be justified in holding this view under these circumstances. But these facts do not, by themselves, make your conviction of your friend's innocence a reasonable one. You stand by her *in the face* of reasonableness, rather than because of it. We will come back in Chapters 3 and 4 to discuss the complex and controversial relation between morality and rationality. For now it might help to have a diagram of the different kinds of ground for a belief:

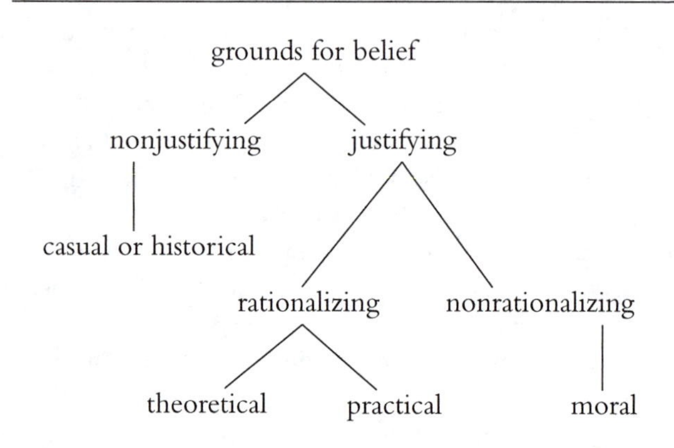

Figure 1: Grounds for Belief. Some grounds for belief justify that belief while others just give causes or their history. Of those that do justify, some make that belief rational, while others do not. Rationalizing justifications for a belief might either be theoretical or practical, while an example of a nonrationalizing justification for a belief is a moral justification. A given belief might have a moral, practical, and theoretical justification, or it might have two of these three.

In the rest of this chapter we will focus on how one might show a belief to be rational, either practically or theoretically; we will also ask what it is for an action to be rational. It is in this phenomenon of rationality that the notion of a compelling argument has its home. However, just to forestall distracting worries, I should make two clarifications. First, when a ground rationalizes a belief or an action, that doesn't mean that the person whose belief or action is thus justified has deceived herself. In contemporary English, describing someone as rationalizing his beliefs or actions is often meant as a criticism: "Bob's always rationalizing driving home after parties by saying he can hold his liquor perfectly well." However, we will be using the term in a nonpejorative way. When some ground rationalizes a belief or action, that makes the belief or action a genuinely, rather than a speciously, reasonable thing to believe or do.

Second, we have said that giving a causal or historical ground for a belief does not by itself show that belief to be justified. This is different from saying that giving a causal or historical ground shows that belief to be *unjustified;* that is, something that one ought to give up. Every belief has a history, and many beliefs are justified. However, just citing a causal or historical basis for a belief does not *show* it to be justified. Similarly, a moral ground for a belief does not rationalize that belief. This is not, however, to say that citing a moral ground shows a belief to be *irrational.* That belief might still be rational for some other reason. Simply because one form of support does not succeed, we can't infer that no other support could.

What Is an Argument?

An *argument,* as we shall use the term, is a line of reasoning purporting to establish a certain thesis. That line of reasoning purports to establish that thesis as theoretically rational in light of the ground given. An argument as defined here need not involve rudeness, flying dishes, or the raising of voices. Op-ed pages in newspapers, lawyers, judges, policy makers, politicians, and often even advertisements make heavy use of arguments—some good, some bad—and it takes skill to tell the good ones from the rest. A first step in learning to discern the difference is to see that any argument comprises a set of propositions (such as "All people are created equal," or "Life begins at conception"). That set of propositions can be divided into two: First there are the *premises,* and then there is the *conclusion.* The premises are intended as justification for the conclusion, which is the thesis that the author aims to establish. Given what we have just said, each argument will contain at least two propositions, although many contain considerably more. Here is an example:

> Although by definition the unconscious patient cannot tell you whether he perceives pain, available data suggest that he may; therefore you cannot know that he doesn't.[1]

The sentence before the semicolon is the premise. What comes after the semicolon is the conclusion. Expressions like "therefore," "ergo," "after all," "so," "it follows that," and "hence" often signal that what follows them will be a conclusion drawn from previously stated premises. Beware, however, that some arguments first state the conclusion to be established and then give the premises later, as in,

> If a man say, I love God, and hateth his brother, he is a liar: for he that loveth not his brother whom he hath seen, how can he love God whom he hath not seen?[2]

In English, one often sees expressions that signal that what is about to come is meant as a reason for the conclusion that has already been stated. Among such expressions are "for," "after all," and "since."

Many arguments have more than one premise, as in the following example:

> To attract new residents, center cities need to provide the amenities that suburbs and edge cities advertise: affordable housing, high-quality education, day care and after-school programs. Unfortunately, most city governments no longer possess the budgets or the tax bases to fully support their social infrastructures. Proper urban planning and design thus require a federal commitment.[3]

The first step in analyzing an argument is to ask yourself what its premises and conclusions are. Once you have done that you can ask whether the argument is any good. To ask this latter question effectively, however, you have to ask two further questions that are quite distinct from one another. The first question has to do with what logicians call validity: let us say that an argument is *valid* just in case, if the premises are true then the conclusion must be true as well. That is, there is no way for all the premises to be true and the conclusion

[1] M. P. McQuillen, "Can People Who Are Unconscious Perceive Pain?" *Issues in Law and Medicine* 6 (1991): 383.

[2] 1 John 4:20 (King James Version).

[3] E. Sclar and N. Aries, "Pulse of the City," *The Sciences* (Nov./Dec. 1992): 44–49.

false. An argument is *invalid* just in case it is not valid. (There is no middle ground between being valid and being invalid; an argument is always either one or the other.) Warning: This definition of validity is not the same as our everyday notion of validity. According to the everyday notion, a valid argument is persuasive, but here validity is only one component of a persuasive argument.

Let me explain. According to our definition, an argument can be valid even if some or all of its premises are false. For instance, the following argument is valid according to our definition of validity even though both premises are false:

All ten-legged creatures have wings.
All spiders have ten legs.

All spiders have wings.

The argument is valid because if the premises *were* true the conclusion would have to be true as well. This is equivalent to saying that there's no possible situation in which the premises are all true and the conclusion false. Notice that this argument is valid in spite of the fact that both the premises and the conclusion are false.

It should be clear that even though the above argument is valid according to our definition of validity, the argument above by no means shows that believing the conclusion that all spiders have wings is theoretically rational. Validity is just a component of arguments that show belief in their conclusion to be theoretically rational, but validity cannot stand on its own. To home in on a better account of a persuasive argument, you might suggest that persuasive arguments need to have true premises. That's a promising suggestion. However, just as an argument's validity doesn't make belief in its conclusion theoretically rational, an argument's having true premises doesn't do so either. Why? Because an argument can be unconvincing even if all its premises are true, as in:

If I owned all the gold in Fort Knox, I'd be rich.
I don't own all the gold in Fort Knox.

I'm not rich.

Even though the premises are true, the speaker might be rich for reasons other than those stated in the premises. Hence knowing that the premises are true does not make it theoretically rational to believe the argument's conclusion. So, just like validity, requiring true premises won't stand on its own as a condition for cogent arguments. What else might we try? How about combining both requirements we've considered into one, and maintain that cogent arguments must both be valid *and* have true premises? That is precisely how we'll frame our definition of soundness: An argument is *sound* just in case it is valid and it has all true premises. An argument is *unsound,* or a *fallacy,* otherwise. That means that even if one of an argument's premises is not true, the argument will be unsound. Here is an example of a sound argument:

All mammals have lungs.
All whales are mammals.

All whales have lungs.

According to our definition, if an argument is sound it must be valid as well, but the validity of an argument does not guarantee its soundness. The sound arguments, then, are a subclass of the valid arguments.

It is often very difficult to know whether a given argument fits our definition of a sound argument, because it is often difficult to know whether all of a bunch of propositions serving as premises in that argument are true. Those premises might be plausible, and they might have a probability greater than one-half. But neither of these two conditions, nor even each of these two conditions together, is enough to show that all the premises are true. Here's where things can get a bit subtle. Suppose you're assessing an argument containing a premise that you think *might* be true, but you just don't know one way or another. The presenter of the argument, Hector, might say, "Look, unless you can show that the premise you're worried about is false, you can't show that my argument isn't sound. So you'll have to concede that it is."

You might feel obliged to concede the conclusion of Hector's argument here, but if you do so, you've fallen for a trick. It is true that in the above situation you don't know that any of Hector's premises is untrue. So according to our definition you don't know that the argument is unsound. However, that doesn't mean that you know that the argument is sound. Hector has set up a false dilemma for you. What you should say in reply to him is that until you know all the premises are true, you don't know that the argument is sound, and thus you don't know whether it establishes its conclusion. Pending further information about the premises, you're within your rights to remain neutral on the question whether the argument is sound, and thus within your rights to remain neutral on the question whether it establishes its conclusion. Tell Hector he should keep on trying.

Philosophers work hard to develop sound arguments in favor of positions concerning free will, the relation between mind and body, what makes an action right, and many other topics. When you try to convince someone else, or even yourself, of a controversial position in any area, you should aim for a sound argument. Likewise, in criticizing the arguments of others your aim should be to see whether their arguments are sound. One way of showing that someone's argument is not sound is to show that it is not valid. The other way is to show that one or more of the premises are false. As we've just seen, you can also challenge an argument by raising doubts as to whether all of its premises are true. If you can disprove or reasonably doubt any of the premises, you will have found a reasonable basis for doubting the soundness of the argument even if it is valid. Once you acquire skills in formulating good arguments and criticizing the arguments of others, you can apply those skills in an unlimited variety of domains.

Fallacies of Theoretical Rationality

Our definition of a sound argument is correct as far as it goes, but it is quite abstract. In addition to knowing this general definition it will be useful to be aware of a handful of fallacies commonly found in daily life. With exceptions that I'll note in a moment, these fallacies are unpersuasive because they are invalid. For this reason they can't be sound, either. Familiarity with these common fallacies will help you to apply your knowledge of the general definition of a sound argument to particular cases.

The fallacy of composition

From the premise that a nation is rich, you might be tempted to conclude that all its inhabitants are rich. From the premise that all of the parts of which I am composed are physical, you might be tempted to conclude that I am a purely physical thing. Those conclusions might happen to be true, but they don't *follow* from the premises cited. Arguments that proceed this way are, accordingly, invalid. Why? From the fact that each member of a group has a certain characteristic, it does not follow that the entire group does; nor is it valid to reason in the other direction, from a property of the composite to properties of each, or even any, of its members. Each grain of sand in a dune might be small, but that does not imply that the dune is small. In fact, the sand dune might be quite large. And, of course, from the fact that a dune is quite large, we cannot infer that any of its constituent grains of sand is large. This fallacy may seem too obvious to mention, but in fact it can be tempting; again, one might be tempted to think that because the state is rich, each of its citizens is rich, but that may not be the case. In addition, a state might consist of nothing but rich citizens without the state itself being rich, for it might have a huge national debt but negligible taxes.

Post hoc, ergo propter hoc

A friend might tell you that she prayed for a solution to her life crisis, and, sure enough, a solution came. An advertisement might tell you that Mr. Thomson took the cold medicine, and lo and behold, he was over his cold in twenty-four hours. I solemnly swear that I once read a book about garlic that mentioned proudly that just about everyone with a cold or flu who consumes garlic recovers within two weeks! In all these cases, the implicit reasoning is that the first event not only preceded the second event, it also caused it. This bit of reasoning is surely not justified by the information given. From just the three premises—(1) A occurred, (2) B occurred, and (3) B occurred subsequent to A—we cannot infer that A caused B. You can see this clearly by considering two events, such as A (the hurricane in Malaysia at noon on Tuesday) and B (a dog's barking five minutes later in Nebraska). It is incredibly unlikely that A caused B, and no one who is told of these two events would likely infer that the first caused the second. Priority is never enough, just on its own, to establish causality.

The fallacy of equivocation

Some arguments use a verbal sleight of hand to seem convincing when they're really not. Specifically, such arguments shift between two senses of a word or expression. Here is one that attempts to prove that the soul is not important.

1. The soul is immaterial.
2. Whatever is immaterial is not important.

ergo, 3. The soul is not important.

It should be easy to see that in the first premise "immaterial" is used in a different sense from the way it is used in the second premise. In premise 1 it is used to mean "not made of matter"; in premise 2 it is used to mean "not important." This is a pun, not a valid argument. We can see that the argument is not valid, because the second premise only appears to include souls within its scope. If we keep in mind the "not made of matter" sense in premise 1 and the "not important" sense in premise 2, that appearance immediately vanishes. (You might also doubt whether premise 1 is true, but the fallacious nature of this argument stops it in its tracks. You don't even have to bother to assess the truth of premise 1 to see that the argument fails.)

Our example of a fallacy of equivocation was pretty blatant. Other examples can be a bit less easy to spot. The philosopher Thomas Hill discusses an argument against affirmative action that he summarizes in the following terms:

> Affirmative action, by definition, gives preferential treatment to minorities and women. This is discrimination in their favor and against non-minority males. All discrimination by public institutions is unjust, no matter whether it is the old kind or the newer "reverse discrimination." So all affirmative action programs in public institutions are unjust.[4]

As Hill points out, this argument might seem compelling at first glance, but further reflection reveals that it trades on different senses of "discrimination." In the second sentence, "discrimination" means

[4] Thomas E. Hill, "The Message of Affirmative Action," *Social Philosophy and Policy* 8 (1991): 108–29. Hill formulates the quoted argument in order to challenge it; he does not endorse the reasoning.

"making a distinction." In this "making a distinction" sense, a basketball coach discriminates the adept players from those that are less skilled, and a music teacher discriminates between those students with an ear for music and those without. In both of these cases the discrimination that occurs is morally unobjectionable even when carried out in a public institution.

On the other hand, "discrimination" sometimes has a pejorative meaning, roughly: "making morally indefensible distinctions." An example of discrimination in this latter sense would be holding that some people have no right to vote because of their religious convictions. Now when the third sentence of the above argument claims that discrimination by public institutions is unjust, it must be using "discrimination" in this latter, pejorative, sense, showing that the above argument equivocates between the "making a distinction" sense of "discrimination" in the second sentence and the pejorative sense of the word in the third. The third sentence is true if "discrimination" is used pejoratively, but then it doesn't cover the "making a distinction" sense used in the second sentence. By contrast, the third sentence is clearly doubtful if "discrimination" is used in the "making a distinction" sense. In either case, the argument is not sound.

Ad hominem

An ad hominem argument attempts to rebut a position someone is defending by pointing out some fact about that person that seems to be in tension with their holding that position. For instance a physician might argue that smoking is a danger to one's health, and an investigative reporter might later reveal that the physician is herself a smoker. While this revelation might show a degree of hypocrisy on the physician's part, it does not undermine the strength of her argument. That argument might still provide incontrovertible evidence of the dangers of smoking. That she is herself a smoker in spite of knowing what she does of its dangers, might, in fact, be further evidence of the perils of smoking, since she may be struggling with a powerful addiction.

More generally, a criticism of an argument on ad hominem grounds at most shows that the person whose argument is being criticized is to some extent insincere or inconsistent. That is the point made when we attack a politician who preaches family values while carrying on extramarital affairs, or when we doubt an executive who tells us how environmentally friendly their corporation is while driving a humongous sport utility vehicle. But look back at our definition of a sound argument. Our definition made no reference to the attitudes of the person presenting the argument. In fact, we can assess an argument even if we have no idea who propounded it. Perhaps we will someday find Mayan glyphs that, after we decipher them, turn out to contain an argument. That we have no idea who wrote them does not undermine our ability to assess the argument they express. Accordingly, an ad hominem attack on an argument is at most an attack on the person presenting it, and while it might raise doubts about that person, it leaves their argument unscathed.

Argument from authority

We are often told that some thesis is true because Einstein believed it or because Shakespeare said it. While it is perhaps true that because an acknowledged genius believed something, we have good reason to take it seriously, one cannot argue soundly from that fact itself to the conclusion that it must be true. After all, even the greatest minds make mistakes. Consequently, from the premise that an authority figure believed something, we cannot validly infer that that belief is true.

The above five common fallacies by no means exhaust all possible kinds of fallacious reasoning. There are many others. However, because of its importance, I would like to mention one more way in which an argument can fail to be persuasive, a way that is not captured by our definition of a fallacy.

Begging the question

Some arguments assume, either implicitly or explicitly, what they set out to prove. We say that arguments that do this beg the question. As an example, suppose someone is trying to show that the death penalty is morally unacceptable. He might argue like this:

> Murder is, by definition, morally wrong. However, the death penalty is just judicial murder, carried out by a judge and the legal system rather than by a lone assailant with a pistol. Hence the death penalty is morally wrong.

It may well be true that murder, by definition, is morally wrong. However, calling the death penalty judicial murder[5] is just a roundabout

[5] I borrow the epithet "judicial murder" from H. Prejean, *Dead Man Walking*. New York: Random House, 1993.

way of presupposing that it is morally wrong. It is one thing to describe the death penalty as the intentional putting to death of a person by the legal system. It is quite another to describe it as a form of murder, and the latter characterization is surely not implied by the former. The premise that the death penalty is judicial murder, then, presupposes what is to be established and thus makes the argument question-begging.

An argument whose premises contain or presuppose the conclusion is of course valid since those premises cannot be true without the conclusion being true as well. On the other hand, a question-begging argument is hardly persuasive: If we don't already accept the conclusion, the argument won't convince us to do so, while if we do accept the conclusion, the argument still won't convince us of anything, since one cannot become convinced of what one already believes. Instead, a question-begging argument may be challenged by remarking that we have no reason to accept the premises. Rather than court confusion by extending our definition of "fallacy" to cover this case, I shall leave that definition intact and simply observe that begging the question is one way in which an argument may fail to be persuasive.

The study of fallacies is a rich and rewarding subject, and I encourage you to pursue it in greater depth. I hope that our brief survey, together with your persistence in looking for examples of these and other fallacies in arguments you consider both later in this book and elsewhere, will spark your interest in further study.

What Is Practical Reasoning?

It is important to know how to design an argument that shows belief in its conclusion to be theoretically rational, and to know how to assess an argument that purports to do so. In addition to striving for theoretical rationality in our beliefs, however, we also frequently seek justifications for choices and actions. Many of those justifications seek to establish that a choice or action is prudent or is a practical undertaking, given our options and aims. The study of practical reasoning attempts to clarify how we can use the notion of prudence effectively to guide our choices and actions.

Suppose you are trying to decide what to do when you don't know what the future holds (surely a common situation!). You don't know what the weather is going to be like on the beach a month from now. Should you plan a vacation and risk spending a week inside doing jigsaw puzzles and watching daytime TV? This depends on how you weigh the chances of bad weather against how much you would like or dislike several of the possible consequences. According to the act/state/outcome (ASO) conception of decision making, you organize your reasoning around the following ideas: First of all, distinguish the different *acts* that are available to you (for instance, taking or not taking a beach vacation). Second, consider the different *states* the world might be in (such as there being acceptable weather or there being lousy weather at the beach). Finally, decide how much you would value the *outcomes* of those acts given the different states the world might be in. You might even organize your thoughts by making a little diagram:

Acts	**States**	
	Lousy Weather	Acceptable Weather
Take a Beach Vacation	lost time and money	spend money; good time
Don't Take a Beach Vacation	paid nothing; perhaps some relief	paid nothing; perhaps some regret

The two choices in the left column are the acts available, while the headings of the two columns on the right are the relevant possible states of the world. The remaining boxes are the outcomes of those acts given those two possible states. A given decision situation might involve many more relevant possible states of the world than just two, and many more relevant possible choices than two, but for simplicity let us start with this 2x2 diagram.

After filling the outcome boxes with qualitative information, you might try to describe that information quantitatively. As a first step, try to fill in that information by ordering the outcomes in terms of your preferences. Which outcome would you prefer? Supposing that 4 is your first choice, I assume that the top right outcome would get a 4; the top left outcome would, by contrast, be the worst and so would get a 1; the bottom left seems better than the bottom right, and so the two get a 3 and a 2, respectively. Our table now looks like this:

Acts	**States**	
	Lousy Weather	Acceptable Weather
Take a Beach Vacation	1	4
Don't Take a Beach Vacation	3	2

We are almost done explaining practical rationality under conditions in which you don't know everything about the world, but we have two more steps. Suppose you hear a reliable forecast that the weather at the beach is going to be excellent. That suggests that taking a beach vacation is the rational thing to do. On the other hand, suppose you hear that a major tropical depression is on the way and that heavy rain is forecast for the entire week you had hoped to travel. That suggests you should stay home. That is, how much you like or dislike various outcomes of your actions, given the various states of the world, needs to be balanced against the likelihood of those states. That's why it is not practically rational to buy a lottery ticket just because there is *some chance* that it will be a winning ticket. The question is how likely it is to be a winning ticket, and that likelihood needs to be weighed against the cash you lost in buying it. So let's suppose that after consulting weather data for the area for the last two decades we conclude that the chance of acceptable weather at the beach is 75 percent. We can note this in our decision matrix at the top of each column. Furthermore, we can now derive a weighted sum of the different outcome values relative to the probabilities for different states of the world: just multiply each outcome value by the probability of the relevant state of the world and then add across. The result is known as *subjective expected utility,* as illustrated below:

Acts	**States**		
	Lousy Weather (25%)	OK Weather (75%)	Expected Utility
Take a Beach Vacation	1 x .25 = .25	4 x .75 = 3	.25 + 3 = 3.25
Don't Take a Beach Vacation	3 x .25 = .75	2 x .75 = 1.5	.75 + 1.5 = 2.25

The subjective expected utility of taking the beach vacation is 3.25, while the subjective expected utility of not doing so is only 2.25, so from the point of view of practical rationality the former is more rational than the latter. In this case, take the vacation. The result would, of course, be different for different weather forecasts.

You might be concerned about the use I've made of the act/state/outcome approach to practical rationality because it so radically simplifies both the real choices we have to make and the possible states of the world that face us. After all, there are lots of different ways in which I might take a beach vacation—I could travel by train or by car; I might do a lot of windsurfing or I might not; I might or might not take the dog. Similarly, there seem to be indefinitely many ways in which weather could be lousy or, by contrast, acceptable. According to the ASO theory, however, the number of columns and rows you use to formulate a decision problem depends upon you. In particular, if various forms of lousy weather will make a difference for how you value effects of that the weather on your acts, then distinguish different kinds of lousy weather in the decision matrix. Otherwise, don't bother. Similarly, if the different forms your vacation might take (with or without the family dog; windsurfing or not, etc.) make a difference for how much you value the possible outcomes, then distinguish those forms of vacation in the decision matrix. Otherwise, don't bother.

Now we are ready to say what it means to act rationally. Use, if you like, the act/state/outcome method to develop a decision matrix. Next, calculate, if you like, the subjective expected utility of the different acts available to you, making sure that your probabilities for the different possible states of the world always add up to exactly 1. Then, after your calculation, *choose the act that has the highest subjective expected utility*. If two or more acts are tied for first place in your subjective expected utility ranking, it doesn't matter which one you choose so long as you choose one of them. As Yogi Berra once suggested, "If you come to a fork in the road, take it."

Why did I use the parenthetical, "if you like" in my characterization of rational decision? You could reasonably ask: "Do I have to use a decision matrix when deciding what to do?" To understand the answer to this question, notice that you often reason according to the rules of theoretical rationality without paying any attention to the fact that you're doing so. That is, you can be theoretically rational without spelling out each of your lines of reasoning in terms of premises and a conclusion. So, too, the account we just gave of practical rationality doesn't strictly require that every time you make a choice you have to write out a decision matrix and calculate subjective expected utilities. As we'll see in Chapter 4's discussion of ethics, John Stuart Mill pointed out over a century ago that we often act rationally without performing any calculations. In fact, in some situations it would be positively *irrational* to calculate subjective expected utilities. (Can you think of one?) Some momentous or complex decisions do require that we calculate subjective expected utility, and the theory of practical rationality gives us tools for doing that. Blaise Pascal's famous wager is such an example, and we will discuss it with some care in the next chapter. In other cases, unless you are in the grip of habits that positively violate the theory of practical rationality, the theory says you should do what comes naturally. As we'll see in Chapter 5, that conclusion is supported by recent work in experimental psychology.

Fallacies of Practical Rationality

Just stated on its own, our theory of practical rationality might seem too obvious to discuss. However, many of us act in ways that are not practically rational. As we saw earlier in this chapter, in some cases we might be obliged by a moral duty: Sometimes morality makes us do things that are not in our best interests. However, we all too often make imprudent choices even when morality is not obliging us to do so, and in this section I shall briefly discuss just two common examples.

The gambler's fallacy

People often say that since we haven't had a bad storm in a while, we're due for a big one. Or that since their favorite baseball team has been losing for a while, the team is sure to win pretty soon. This way of thinking assumes that the probability of later events depends on what has happened before. In some cases that is true. For instance, if you are choosing balls from an urn without replacing them, then the probability of a choosing a given color might depend on what you have chosen thus far. However, weather and baseball aren't like that. That there was no storm last month hasn't any effect on the likelihood of a storm this month. Similarly, and unfortunately, that the baseball team lost every game last month doesn't increase their chances of winning this month. Misjudgment of probabilities does not prevent one from calculating subjective expected utilities. However, it does skew one's judgment of the chances of various possible states of the world, and in this way it can result in imprudent choices.

The "person who" fallacy

We often hear stories about a "person who": smoked a pack a day and lived until ninety; never used seatbelts and never had an accident; played the lottery and won big-time, etc. Stories of this sort might be perfectly true, but do they justify not worrying about the health hazards of smoking, or not bothering with seatbelts, or purchasing lottery tickets? No, they don't, and here is why: As the subjective expected utility approach to prudent action shows, the rationality of an action depends not only on how much one would value its possible payoff, but also on how likely that payoff is. Suppose I am about to make dinner. It's possible that if I go to my front porch and do a handstand, someone walking by might decide to give me dinner. That would be really nice, since making dinner takes time and effort. But that doesn't for a moment justify my going to my front porch and doing a handstand. Similarly, the sheer possibility that I could be a chain smoker yet live a long life doesn't make it rational for me to ignore the hazards of smoking. The same goes for not bothering with seatbelts, or for purchasing lottery tickets.

The calculator's fallacy

I've said that a practically rational agent maximizes subjective expected utility. You might think this implies that to be rational you need to draw up a decision matrix every time you are about to make a choice. However, this doesn't follow. Note that if it did follow, you'd never be able to act rationally; in order to choose whether to perform some action A, you'd have to write up a decision matrix. But writing up a decision matrix is itself an action, and so then you'd have to write up a decision matrix to help decide whether to write up a decision matrix! This obviously would go on forever. In fact, given that some decisions have to be made on the fly (a burglar climbing through your window is not likely to give you time to calculate), it would be positively irrational to make a calculation every time you decide how to act. Calculate only when you have time and when the situation is sufficiently complex to justify the details.

In this chapter we've studied reasoning, both theoretical and practical. Although at this point the discussion might still seem quite abstract, in the chapters that follow you will see that the skills that both forms of reasoning require are directly applicable to questions at the heart of philosophy. In the meantime, a good way of testing whether you are building these skills is to try to answer the study questions below.

Study Questions

1. A belief can be theoretically rational without being practically rational, and vice versa. Can you think of a belief that is theoretically rational without being practically rational? Can you think of a belief that is practically rational without being theoretically rational?

2. Can a sound argument have a false conclusion? Please explain your answer.

3. Can an argument be valid even if one of its premises is *necessarily* false, such as "2+2=5"? Please explain your answer.

4. Can an argument be sound even when one of its premises is restated as the conclusion? Please explain your answer.

5. Create your own example of a fallacy of equivocation, then use our definition of validity to show that this argument is not valid.

6. Describe a case in which it would be practically irrational, according to our theory of subjective expected utility, to use a decision matrix or some other formal device to calculate the subjective expected utility of a prospective action.

7. My cousin George never wears seatbelts when he drives. His reason is that it is possible that one day while driving he might go off a bridge or the side of a road and end up at the bottom of a lake or river. In that situation he might also be unable to unbuckle his seatbelt, and so would drown. Is this justification a good use of practical rationality? Please explain your answer.

Suggestions for Further Reading

Logic can be studied either under the rubric of "informal logic" or under that of "symbolic logic." The former is the study of reasoning forms as they occur in English and other natural languages, and it tends to use a minimum of symbolism. The latter is, strictly, a branch of mathematics and is more technically rigorous than informal logic. Symbolic logic is important background not only for advanced work in philosophy, but also for computer science, psychology, linguistics, and mathematics. The following are among the many good texts treating informal logic:

Porter, B. *The Voice of Reason: Fundamentals of Critical Thinking*. Oxford: Oxford University Press, 2002.

Weston, A. *A Rulebook for Arguments.* 3rd ed. Indianapolis: Hackett Publishing Company, 2000.

An excellent introduction to symbolic logic is W. Goldfarb. *Deductive Logic.* Indianapolis: Hackett Publishing Company, 2004.

Another distinguished introduction to symbolic logic using a graphically accessible method known as the "tree method" is R. Jeffrey. *Formal Logic: Its Scope and Limits*. 3rd edition. Indianapolis: Hackett Publishing Company, 2004.

Two accessible introductions to practical rationality are:

Skyrms, B. *Choice and Chance.* 4th edition. Belmont, CA: Wadsworth, 1975.

Resnik, M. *Choices: An Introduction to Decision Theory.* Minneapolis: University of Minnesota Press, 1987.

A more demanding but quite rewarding introduction is R. Jeffrey. *The Logic of Decision*, 2nd edition. Chicago: University of Chicago Press, 1983.

Movies Significant for Logic and Reasoning

Twelve Angry Men (1957), directed by Sidney Lumet.

The Usual Suspects (1995), directed by Bryan Singer.

3. The Greatest Conceivable Being

Now we are ready to plunge into a philosophical question and start skill-building. We will begin with a topic to which nearly everyone has paid some attention at some point, and in the course of which they have done some philosophizing. Many have felt that, on pain of irrationality, we must believe in a divine being. Others have felt that belief in a divine being is positively *irrational.* To simplify our discussion we shall define a divine being as one having all possible perfections. If omnipotence is a perfection then, on the present definition, God has it; if omnibenevolence is a perfection then, on our definition, God has it. To help fix ideas we may refer to God as the GCB, or Greatest Conceivable Being. In so defining God I am trying to abstract away from the specific features that various monotheistic traditions ascribe to their divine being. Christians, Muslims, and Jews, for example, will each say different things about their God. On the other hand, these traditions seem to agree that their God is the greatest conceivable and is perfect in every way. Accordingly, I am hoping my remarks about the GCB will apply to a wide variety of religious traditions.

Our question is, then, Can we have a rational or some other justifying basis for one view or another about the existence of the GCB? By way of further jargon, let's say that one who believes that the GCB exists is a *theist;* one who believes that the GCB does not exist is an *atheist,* and one who is neutral on the issue is an *agnostic.* Evidently there is no fourth option on the question of the existence of the GCB.[1]

For many theists, their beliefs about the GCB are among the most important in their lives. People with rival religious views have killed one another over the issue. Nontheists have been burned alive, tortured, and persecuted in other ways for their failure to believe what theists enjoin

[1] You might ask: "One person might be an agnostic because she has thought about the question and decided to refrain from belief. Another person might be an agnostic simply because she has never considered the issue of the existence of a GCB; perhaps she lives in an isolated society that doesn't discuss religious questions at all. Aren't these two kinds of agnostic quite different?" The answer is, yes, they are quite different, but for present purposes lumping these two kinds of people into the same category will do no harm, and it will help to keep our discussion simple.

them to believe; theists have been treated similarly by others. Even if you are still making up your mind about your religious views, it seems clear that the issue is momentous. So it would seem natural to use reason to settle an issue so important, and our first question shall be whether theism can be justified. As you know from the last chapter, you won't show that your theism is justified by pointing out that you were raised in a deeply religious family; that's a cause, not a justification of your belief. Instead, you might look for a theoretical justification for theism, either by citing evidence or in some a priori way. (In earlier centuries this line of inquiry was called natural religion.) Failing that, you might seek a justification having to do with practical rationality or even morality. We'll consider all three approaches in this chapter.

You might doubt, though, that it's even appropriate to ask whether belief in a GCB can be justified. I've often heard people say that questions of religion, which of course include but are not limited to the existence of a GCB, are subjective. What does this mean? Maybe it means something like what we mean in saying that a preference for chocolate over vanilla ice cream is subjective. Certainly there is no arguing over whether chocolate tastes better than vanilla, because we simply have our preferences on these matters. The question of the existence of the GCB, however, seems different. First of all, while we can see that attempts to give a justification for preferring one ice cream flavor over another would be pointless, can we be sure that attempts to give a justification for one or another belief about the GCB must be pointless as well? As we're about to see, plenty of intelligent people over the centuries have tried to give such justifications. I don't know how one could show that all such attempts were and always will be simply hopeless. Second, recall the enormous consequences that follow from belief in the GCB in one form or another: People have killed others and sacrificed themselves for religion; entire nations have gone to war over such matters, and many choices that confront us daily are deeply influenced by our theological convictions if we have them. Would you be willing to fight to the death over an issue that is at bottom "subjective"?

I'm in no position to prove that the question of the existence of the GCB is not subjective. The only way I know to do that would be to provide a sound argument either in favor of theism or in favor of atheism. As we're about to see, although many such lines of reasoning are intriguing and raise fascinating questions, such an argument has proven elusive. On the other hand, I also don't know of a sound argument showing that no theological or atheological argument can be found. As a matter of fact, I have yet to meet a person who seems sincerely to believe that the question of theism is entirely subjective. In every case in which I've met a person who *claims* to hold this, I've found that he has reasons for his position after all. For instance, to a theist who claims that all religious belief is subjective, one might ask, "Well then, why do you believe in the GCB rather than in, say, elves or, for that matter, Elvis (particularly as Elvis gets more attention in supermarket checkout magazines than do either elves or the GCB)?" Among the answers that I have heard to this question are, "You'd have to be silly to believe in Elvis or elves!" (implying there's more *evidence* in favor of the GCB?); "The GCB is simply greater and more worthy of worship!" (implying there is a *reason* for preferring to believe in one rather than the others?); and so on. Once we are clear what it means to say that an issue is subjective, it seems doubtful that the GCB's existence is like that, and intelligent people are aware of this in spite of some protestations to the contrary. At any rate, let's adopt the working hypothesis that the existence of the GCB is an objective, rather than a subjective, matter, and see where it leads us.

In addition to the view that questions about the existence of a GCB are subjective, one often hears that such questions are matters of the heart, not of the head. Here is an analogy: Imagine Portia trying to decide whether to marry Hunter. She may try following Ben Franklin's method of drawing up a column of "pros" and another column of "cons" to decide the matter. However, you might suggest to her that too much thinking can get in the way of listening to her heart, which may be the most eloquent indication of the viability of a life with Hunter. Perhaps the choice to marry someone is best not decided in terms of rationality, but instead by asking whether doing so "feels right." However, following one's "gut" is still a way of being rational, or at least of trying to be. Recall, from Chapter 2, our distinction between theoretical and practical rationality. Since our gut feelings are often reliable indicators of our assessments of a situation as well as of other people, following one's gut on a matter such as marriage can be a way of acting in one's best interests. That is, acting on one's gut instincts can be a way of being practically rational. So too, if belief in the GCB is a matter of the heart not the mind, then that may be to say that it is an issue falling into the domain of practical rather than theoretical rationality. In that case it will still be an issue apt for rational assessment. Matters of the heart do not, that is, necessarily fall outside the realm of reason.

In this chapter we will distinguish between theological arguments, which aim to show that theism is either rational or moral, and atheological arguments, which aim to show that atheism is rational or moral, and we will consider a few of each kind.

Theological Arguments

The argument from design

You've got to be impressed by the variety of complex and sophisticated natural phenomena around us. Stories of how the spider spins its web, of how the bat pursues its prey, of how the eye and brain conspire to produce vision, of how stars are born in nebulae, of how subatomic particles behave, are simply awe inspiring. Some of these phenomena seem to show organisms that are complexly and intricately designed for their purpose, and this suggests the possibility of an intelligent designer responsible for it all. One of the most famous of all theological arguments is, in fact, that the complexity and apparent design in nature show that there must be an intelligent, sentient designer; that is, a designer who is not only intelligent but also aware of the things it is designing and how it is designing them. One famous proponent of that argument was the English philosopher and theologian William Paley (1743–1805). A very simple version of his argument, known as the argument from design, follows:

1. The natural world shows considerable complexity and apparent design.
2. The only possible explanation of this complexity and apparent design in the natural world is that the natural world was produced by an intelligent, sentient designer.

---

3. Therefore, there must be an intelligent, sentient designer responsible for the complexity and apparent design in the natural world.

Premise 1 seems beyond dispute. You just need to open your eyes to discern an amazing array of complexity in nature, and much of it *seems* to be designed for specific purposes whether or not it really is. (That is, in referring to "apparent design" in the world we are not assuming that any part of nature really was designed.) Further, premises 1 and 2 together do imply 3, the conclusion. That is, in terms of the concept of validity given in Chapter 2, the argument is valid: *If* the premises are true, *then* the conclusion must be as well. This leaves the question whether we should accept premise 2. (If we don't accept premise 2, then we will have no reason to think the argument sound.) After all, is an intelligent, sentient designer the *only* possible explanation for the complexity and apparent design that we see around us?

One of the most earthshaking scientific theories of the last two centuries was evolution by natural selection (ENS for short). If we assume that genes are the carriers of an organism's traits, that those genes are passed on to its host organism's offspring, and that in a given population there is a certain amount of random genetic variation, then we can account for the organisms' existence as well as for many of their features. We do this by hypothesizing that their particular, genetically endowed characteristics gave their ancestors a survival advantage. That survival advantage increased each ancestor's ability to survive, thereby its ability to reproduce, and thereby the likelihood of its passing on its genes to offspring. On the whole, the faster, stronger, more malleable creatures have tended to survive, passing on their genes and hence their advantages to their offspring. On this theory of evolution by natural selection, Mother Nature is a designer. She may even be intelligent, although there is no reason to think she is sentient: Mother Nature is not conscious and does not have plans. ENS nevertheless purports to explain the evolution of vision to the sophisticated visual systems we now find in the animal kingdom, as well as the evolution of other awe-inspiring biological phenomena.

Contemporary evolutionary biologists disagree with one another over the exact form that a theory of ENS should take. In addition, many people take ENS to be relatively speculative, due, among other things, to the paucity of available information in the fossil record. We do not know, for example, when and under what circumstances hominids began to speak sophisticated natural languages such as Hopi or Swahili. Those issues need not detain us, however, for remember that premise 2 contends that the *only* possible explanation of the extent of complexity and organization in the natural world is an intelligent, sentient designer. But now we see that ENS is another possible explanation. True, if ENS were conclusively refuted, then it would no longer be a possible explanation. However, it has not been conclusively refuted, and until it has, it remains a possible explanation of premise 1. ENS, then, undermines premise 2, showing that Paley's argument is valid but not sound.

People sometimes say that ENS doesn't really pose a challenge to the argument from design because ENS is "just a theory." This remark does not advance discussion. If the critic means that ENS goes beyond the immediate data to account for that data, then it is in no way inferior to quantum mechanics, special relativity, plate tectonics, or the idea that germs spread disease. These are theories too. In fact, they're all probably true, so calling them "just theories" doesn't undermine them at all. On the other hand, if, by calling ENS "just a theory," the critic means that it has not yet been conclusively established, we can agree and refer them to the point we made in the previous paragraph, that ENS need not be conclusively established to pose a threat to the argument from design.

ENS offers an account of the complexity and apparent design in the organic world. It does not offer an account of the complexity and apparent design that might be found in the inorganic world. A defender of the argument from design might hold on to his argument by focusing just on the inorganic, but he will need to make it plausible that the inorganic world shows so much complexity and apparent design that it requires an explanation in terms of sentience. A hurricane is incredibly complex, but nothing in this complex storm system calls out for an account in terms of an intelligent designer. Likewise for a solar system: The system of planets and other debris orbiting our sun might look like it is the product of intelligent design, but as astrophysics progresses, it offers the hope of a satisfying account in purely physical terms of how our solar system formed. While astrophysicists are still working out the details of how stars are formed in nebulae and of how planets are formed as a result of that process, we are certainly in no position to claim that an intelligent designer—sentient or otherwise—is the only possible explanation of how these processes work. Similarly for other inorganic processes.

One might also respond with a revision of the above argument. Let's concede, you might suggest, that the thesis that the natural world was produced by an intelligent, sentient designer is not the only possible explanation of apparent complexity and design. We've now seen that there are other possible explanations, such as ENS. On the other hand, you might suggest, even if it's not the *only*, this thesis is the *best* of those available, and so is still worthy of our credence.

It should be easy to see that "best" can mean lots of things, only some of which are relevant to establishing a conclusion. A hypothesis can be the best available by being the most pleasant: A child's idea that the Tooth Fairy exchanged his recently lost tooth for a dollar is more pleasant than the idea that it was the work of a groggy parent. So in a sense the Tooth Fairy is the best explanation of the missing tooth and the dollar. Yet this way of being a best hypothesis is not what is at issue when we discuss a GCB. Instead, what makes a hypothesis best is that it is most strongly supported by the evidence. So the question is whether the evidence, either the evidence cited by the argument from design or evidence from elsewhere, does make theism the best-supported theory among the alternatives.

The answer appears to be that it does not. To see why, consider that when we offer a theory to account for data, we tend to prefer the theory with the fewest commitments possible. If two theories T_1 and T_2 are just alike except that T_2 contains a postulate that explains none of the relevant phenomena, we generally prefer T_1. T_1 is a better theory under these circumstances. Parsimony is a virtue in theory construction just as it is a virtue in your personal finances. In fact, T_1 might be a reigning theory for a while, until it is challenged by a person who shows how some new theory T_3 can explain all that T_1 does but make do with even fewer postulates. Then T_3 is an even better theory than T_1.

How does this bear on the GCB? Recall that the GCB by definition has features that don't seem to help account for the apparent complexity and design we find in the natural world: Omnipotence and omnibenevolence are two of those features. You can account for apparent complexity and design just by supposing a being powerful enough (not even omnipotent) to create it, and decent enough (not even omnibenevolent) to have reason to do so. Omniscience seems like an explanatory fifth wheel, too. If that's right, then your theory, (T_1), that the GCB created and designed everything, can be bettered by a theory (T_2) that simply supposes a being powerful enough to create what we see around us and perhaps decent enough to have reason to do so. That just shows, however, that theory T_1, that the GCB created and designed everything, is not the best explanation of the apparent complexity and design in the world around us.

Well, you might say, beggars can't be choosers. Might the argument from design still establish a Very Great Being (VGB), if not the Greatest Conceivable Being? If so, then maybe we could find other arguments to shore up properties of the VGB so that it becomes the GCB as well? For instance, as we'll see below, many have thought that certain facts about morality could show a Very Great Being to be omnibenevolent too.

This many-pathed way to the GCB is an intriguing strategy, and by considering other arguments for the GCB later in this chapter we will see if it will work. Let's keep in mind, however, that ENS even challenges the ability of the argument from design to establish a Very Great Being. We know that the VGB hypothesis is not the only possible explanation of the apparent complexity and design we see in the world around us. Further, we haven't found any reason to think that the VGB hypothesis is better than the hypothesis of ENS. If that's right, then we have no reason to conclude that the VGB hypothesis is the best explanation of the available data. That doesn't mean it is not true. It may be. What it does mean is that we'll have to keep searching if we want to find a rational basis for belief in a GCB or anything like it. So let's keep looking.

The cosmological argument

Perhaps you agree that the argument from design is less powerful than it appeared at first glance. The argument from design will certainly need help from elsewhere if we are to find a rational basis for belief in a GCB. Now, however, you might point out that we have other facts crying out for an explanation, such as that there is a certain amount of carbon in the universe, or that there are a certain number of galaxies. What accounts for such facts? For that matter, what accounts for the fact that there was a big bang in the first place rather than nothing existing at all? These questions suggest a new form of argument, the cosmological argument.

The cosmological argument starts with a question about where everything around us might have come from. Surely, one asks, there must have been something that got everything going, for instance, by creating the conditions for the occurrence of the big bang. That something must in some way be special, since if it were just another bit of matter one would be entitled to ask where it came from. One way of reading the philosopher and theologian Saint Thomas Aquinas (1225–74), for instance, suggests that according to him there must have been a "first mover" responsible for all subsequent events, since it is hard to see how else there could be anything at all. He writes,

> . . . whatever is moved must be moved by another. If that by which it is moved be itself moved, then this also must be moved by another, and that by another again. But this cannot go on to infinity, because then there would be no first mover, and consequently no other mover, seeing that subsequent movers move only inasmuch as they are moved by the first mover. ("The Five Ways")

Aquinas assumes as obvious that the only way anything could move is if it were moved by a first mover; later in this passage he claims that that first mover must be somehow special.

Do we feel sure that events cannot recede back into infinity? Perhaps for any given event e_0, that event was caused by e_{-1}, which was in turn caused by e_{-2}, and so on back infinitely. This "infinite causal regression" does not seem absolutely impossible. Nothing in principle seems to rule out this possibility. If an infinite causal regression is possible, though, then it would seem as well that each event e_i would have an explanation in terms of an event e_{i-1}, and yet there would be no first event that started the entire chain of events. A series of events stretching infinitely back in time in this way is known as an *infinite causal regression*. In principle, it seems, we have no way of being sure that every chain of causes must have an initial element. Thus it would seem that Aquinas' line of reasoning is not cogent because it assumes, without basis, that there can be no infinite causal regression.

Might there be another way of supporting theism that improves upon Aquinas? The English philosopher and theologian Samuel Clarke (1675–1729) attempted to improve upon Aquinas' line of reasoning with an argument that leaves open the possibility of an infinite causal regression.[2] That is, he provided an argument that, unlike Aquinas' argument, does not assume that there can be no such thing as an infinite causal regression. First let us define a *dependent being* as any entity (planet, coffee cup, neutrino) that has the reason for its existence outside itself. By contrast we may define an *independent being* as any being that has the reason for its existence inside itself. (We are not assuming that there are any independent beings; this is just a definition, just as I might define a "scrump" as a warm-blooded reptile without having any idea if a scrump exists.) Then Clarke suggests that there couldn't be *just* an infinite causal regression of dependent beings. Just as there couldn't be a peninsula without surrounding water, or a mountain without a valley, so too, Clarke argues, if there is an infinite

[2] From *A Demonstration of the Being and Attributes of God, and Other Writings*, E. Vailati, ed. New York: Cambridge University Press, 1998.

causal regression of dependent beings, then there has to be something else as well, and in particular that something else would have to be an independent rather than a dependent being. The argument starts with a premise that is put forth as a supposition, something you are asked to accept for a moment so that you can see that if it *were* true, it would yield an error. This in turn shows that the premise in question is not true. Clarke reasons somewhat as follows:

1. Suppose (merely for the sake of argument) there is nothing but an infinite causal regression of dependent beings, or an ICRDB for short.
2. There must be some explanation of the existence of the entire ICRDB.
3. That explanation can't exist outside of the ICRDB.
4. Nor can that explanation exist inside of the ICRDB.
5. So the ICRDB exists without any explanation at all.
6. But this contradicts our second premise.

So, 7. The supposition in premise 1 must be false.

The structure of the above-displayed line of reasoning is known as a *reductio ad absurdum:* We start with supposing something, show that supposition leads to an absurdity, and then infer that the supposition in question must be false. Clarke tries this with the assumption that the universe is nothing but an ICRDB. If he can show that this assumption implies a falsehood, he will show that this assumption cannot be true. If premise 1 is false, that might either be because the universe is nothing but a finite causal regression of dependent beings or because the universe has at least one independent being in it. Clarke thinks that everything must have an explanation, and so he would reject the first case, namely, that the universe is a finite causal regression of dependent beings. (Its first element would have no cause, and hence no explanation at all.) Clarke concludes that the universe must have at least one independent being in it.

Why does premise 4 follow from the premises above it? Because any alleged reason for the existence of the ICRDB that is inside that series must either be a dependent being or some set of these dependent beings. Assume for now that this set is finite, so that it only contains finitely many dependent beings, and perhaps only one. Then that set will have a first member and a last (not necessarily distinct) member. Accordingly, while that set of dependent beings might account for the existence of members of the ICRDB subsequent to it, it cannot account for members of the ICRDB that are prior to it. After all, it doesn't seem that one event could be responsible for another that precedes it. It follows that the finite set of events inside the ICRDB cannot account for the existence of the entire ICRDB.

One infinite set can be a subset of another. For instance, the set of even integers is a subset of the integers, and both are infinite. What, then, if the reason for the existence of the ICRDB is a subset of the ICRDB while still being infinite? Clarke needs to consider this case, too. He would apparently say that while this subset itself explains the existence of the entire ICRDB, it is itself in need of explanation. Because of this, either in light of this need to account for this infinite subset or to account for an infinite subset of this infinite subset . . . and so forth, we will eventually "bottom out" at a finite subset, which itself is in need of explanation. Hence Clarke seems justified in saying that if the ICRDB needs an explanation in terms of something distinct from it, that thing cannot itself be inside it, either finite or infinite.

Are you convinced? On what basis does Clarke hold premise 2 (there must be some reason why the ICRDB exists)? Its only justification seems to be the larger assumption that everything exists for a reason. Is that assumption something that we know to be true? If so, we don't know it by having done an exhaustive survey of all the things that there are. Or do we know it a priori, independent of experience, like the way in which we know that 2+2=4 or that the interior angles of a triangle add up to 180 degrees? Neither proposal seems quite right.

Even if we accept the idea that the ICRDB exists for a reason, it doesn't follow from this that there must be one *single* reason that accounts for the whole thing. Perhaps we can account for the ICRDB piecemeal? Here is a suggestion put forth by Cleanthes, an interlocutor in David Hume's *Dialogues Concerning Natural Religion:*

> In such a chain [an ICRDB], too, or succession of objects, each part is caused by that which preceded it, and causes that which succeeds it. Where then is the difficulty? But the *whole,* you say, wants a cause. I answer that the uniting of these parts into a whole, like the uniting of several distinct countries into one kingdom, or several distinct members into one body, is performed merely by an arbitrary act of the mind, and has no influence on the nature of things. Did I show you the particular cause of each individual in a collection of twenty particles of matter, I should think it very unreasonable should you afterwards ask me

> what was the cause of the whole twenty. This is sufficiently explained in explaining the cause of the parts. (*Dialogues,* p. 56)

Cleanthes suggests that once you've accounted for the existence of each element in a totality, there is no *further* question of how to account for that totality. Suppose that you see four long distance runners at various times as you walk along a country road. Suppose further that you found out later why each one was there, on that particular road, running at that particular time. One was there because this is her usual running route and schedule; another is there because he had never tried this route before and wanted to give it a go on this particularly beautiful day; a third is there because his car broke down, he has an appointment, and has no other way of getting to it; the fourth is there because he was hoping to have a conversation with you, knew he'd find you here at this hour, and thought running would be a fun and healthy way to meet you. Now you know why each of those runners was on the road at this time. Hume's Cleanthes' point is that once you have this information, there is no further question to ask, such as, Why is the entire group of them here, rather than some other group or no group at all? Once you've accounted for the presence of all the elements in a series, there is nothing left to account for. The same goes for the stages of the universe, even if they form an infinite causal regression.

Let us call this *Hume's principle:* Once you have explained the properties of each element in a totality, you have explained the features of the totality as well. If Hume's principle is correct, then Clarke's demand, that there must be some reason for the existence of the entire ICRDB that is over and above a piecemeal explanation of each of its components, is one that we may reject without simply being irresponsible. Rather, if Hume's principle is correct, then Clarke is placing an unreasonable demand on explanations, and if that is the case then his revised version of the cosmological argument does not succeed: Since premise 2 is questionable, we have not been given reason to think Clarke's argument is sound.

The ontological argument

So far we've tried two attempts to show that theism is theoretically rational. Our first attempt required that we assume that the only possible explanation of the complexity and apparent design in the world is that it was made by an intelligent, sentient designer. This assumption seems questionable because there is another possible explanation: the theory of evolution by natural selection. We then noticed that for ENS to be so much as possible, matter would have to exist. Where could that matter come from? That question forms the basis of the cosmological argument. We've found that this argument runs into trouble once we consider the possibility that the chain of events forms an infinite causal regression. That may seem unlikely, but it is possible, and the proponent of the cosmological argument has no way of ruling it out. Samuel Clarke makes an ingenious attempt to show that even if there is an infinite causal regression, there still has to be an independent being. However, we found no reason to think his argument sound.

Might there be another way to show that theism is theoretically rational? Here is an argument attempting to show that from the very *concept* of the GCB we may infer that God exists. We know that by definition God is the GCB. Being the greatest conceivable implies that one has all possible perfections: If there is a perfection that a being lacks, then that being is not the greatest conceivable. Furthermore, at least for things that are good, it would seem that they are more perfect if they exist than if they don't. For instance, imagine your dream date, the most wonderful person you can imagine going out with. You get to pick the person's gender, hairstyle, hobbies, musical tastes, and so forth. Now suppose someone tells you, "There's only one little problem. To the best of our knowledge that person does not exist." You'd be disappointed. You would probably think that dream dates would be even more wonderful if they existed. If so, then perhaps this is enough to get you to see that good things are more perfect if they exist than if they do not exist.[3] Now we have all the premises that we need for the ontological argument:

1. God is the GCB.
2. God has all possible perfections.
3. Existence is a perfection.
4. God has the property of existence,

ergo, 5. God exists.

Premise 1 just states a definition. It does not assume that "God" refers to anything. In fact, none of premises 1–4 assumes that "'God" refers to

[3] I owe this example to Richard Gale.

anything at all. Those lines of the argument just spell out the definition of the GCB and the consequences of that definition. We owe this argument to Saint Anselm (1033–1109), a theologian and philosopher who was also Archbishop of Canterbury. Anselm summarizes this line of thought by saying that so long as the GCB exists in your understanding, that is, so long as you can form a coherent idea of the GCB, you must acknowledge that the GCB exists in reality as well.

A monk who was a contemporary of Anselm's, Gaunilo, held that this argument must have gone wrong somewhere. Gaunilo's point was that if the argument was a good one, it could just as easily be used to prove the existence of a Greatest Conceivable Island. After all, a GCI has all possible islandly perfections, such as maximally white sand, perfect surfing waves, delicious coconuts, and so forth. So too, it would be better for that island to exist than for it not to exist. It is easy to see how the conclusion would follow. Gaunilo's point, then, is that if Anselm's argument were any good, it would also prove the existence of the GCI; but of course there is no such GCI. Hence, Gaunilo concludes, Anselm's argument is no good.

Gaunilo in effect lampoons Anselm's argument without quite putting his finger on where Anselm's argument goes wrong. Moreover, Anselm eventually found a reply to Gaunilo by pointing out that unlike the concept of a GCB, the concept of a GCI is in fact not well defined. Let's return to that island. Unlike God, the island is a physical object with quantitative, not just qualitative features. However, maximal perfection does not seem to make sense for something with quantitative features. To see why, notice that for any number N of grains of sand on the imagined island, for instance, the island would be even greater if it had just one more, N+1; likewise for palm trees, coconuts, and surfable waves. Anselm's point is that the GCI is not well defined, just as the concept of the largest integer is not well defined. By contrast, we have, at least thus far, no reason to doubt that the concept of the GCB is well defined. (Later in this chapter we discuss the paradox of the stone, which does raise this doubt.)

Anselm, then, seems to fend off Gaunilo's challenge. Should we be convinced, therefore, by his argument? Many people have been convinced of it. I suggest that we do well to scrutinize the idea that existence is a perfection. After all, the "dream date" example might be challenged. While it might be better *for you* if your dream date exists, that does not show that existing makes the person in question more perfect. (Consider this case: A Goth-rock Satan-worshiper might justifiably feel that it would be better for them if Satan existed. However, this wouldn't prove the existence of the Greatest Conceivable Evil Being.)

Perhaps, then, it is not so clear that existence is a perfection. Instead, another way of formulating an ontological argument begins with the thought that the GCB is possible. Most nontheists will be happy to agree that it is possible that the GCB exists. Yet, the theist will now point out, a GCB couldn't just exist in some possible situation. If the GCB were to be merely possible, it would then be contingent, subject to outrageous fortune—thus not the greatest conceivable. Instead, to be the Greatest Conceivable, the GCB would have to exist not just possibly, but necessarily. But, of course, if a being exists necessarily, then we can be quite sure that it exists. Hence, if the GCB is possible, then it is necessary and thus actual.

That's a big "if." A skeptic might have reasons for doubting that the GCB really is possible. Perhaps contradiction lurks in the very concept of the GCB—a question we shall address momentarily. Again, even if you grant that the GCB is possible, you might point out that this new line of reasoning replaces the premise that existence is a perfection with the weaker premise that *necessary existence* is a perfection. Though weaker, it might still be doubted along lines similar to those that raised our doubts about the stronger premise. Nonetheless, I hope you'll agree that the project of formulating a persuasive ontological argument is a tantalizing one.

Pascal's wager

You may have followed all of the foregoing arguments, acknowledging their pitfalls as well, and come to the conclusion that none of them quite establishes that theism is theoretically rational. At the same time it might seem to you that belief in the GCB is reasonable, because even if there is a slight *chance* that God exists, one does well to hedge one's bets. The French philosopher-mathematician Blaise Pascal (1623–62), in his *Pensées,* espouses just this line of reasoning. He contends first of all that "reason" cannot decide the matter whether God exists. By this I take him to mean that we are not in a position to show that theism is either theoretically rational or theoretically irrational. Pascal observes that nevertheless one cannot hide from the choice whether or not to believe in God. As we noted at the beginning of this chapter, there seems no other choice but to be a theist, an atheist, or an agnostic. Given, however, that there is a fact of the matter as to what will become of us after death (either we will achieve eternal bliss or something else), any choice we make among these three options is going to have consequences.

Pascal suggests that even if there is only a very small chance that there is a GCB, it is still rational to be a theist. He reasons that the amount of value you would gain from an eternity of blissful union with a GCB is so great that it swamps this small probability. For consider this decision matrix:

	The GCB Exists (1%)	**The GCB Does Not Exist (99%)**	**Expected Utility**
Choose Theism	eternal reward: 10,000	wasted piety?: 100	100 + 99 = 199
Choose Nontheism	eternal damnation: 1	no piety: 50	49.5 + .01 = 49.51

As this matrix suggests, if you choose theism and the GCB exists, then you'll apparently receive an eternal reward; hence the very high utility of 10,000. If you choose theism and the GCB does not exist, then perhaps you've "wasted piety" by being religious rather than living an unfettered life. For instance, you might not have had to spend all those Sunday mornings in church. If, moving to the next row, you choose nontheism and there is a GCB after all, then you'll evidently receive eternal damnation. That doesn't sound like much fun; hence a very low utility for the outcome of 1. On the other hand if you choose nontheism only to find that the GCB doesn't exist after all, then you won't have wasted your time being pious; on the other hand you won't get any eternal reward either. That's why a utility of 50 might be about right. Please note, however, that all four of these utilities are my own guesses about how typical readers will feel about the various outcomes. You need to fill in these values for yourself to see how Pascal's reasoning would apply to you.

After filling out the four utility values in the above matrix in a way that reflects how you would rate the four possible outcomes, you may well conclude that the matrix shows that the expected utility of theism is greater than that of nontheism (which includes both atheism and agnosticism), and by a good margin. This argument is amazing in that it assumes the probability of a GCB existing to be only 1 percent. That is a pretty innocuous assumption. This small probability is weighed against the immense value we would presumably find in an eternal heavenly reward. Pascal's point is that even if there is a very small probability of a GCB existing, it is still practically rational to choose theism. (Of course, the probability of a GCB could go even lower depending upon how much you value the four possible outcomes.) In fact, I'll bet you can find atheists who would admit that there is some small chance that they are wrong, and hence some small chance that the GCB exists. Pascal's argument seems to show that it is practically rational even for such people to become theists.

It is also surprising that one need not even value an eternal reward, as described in the top left quadrant at 10,000, for the argument to work. As you can see from the large difference in expected utility between choosing theism and choosing nontheism, that 10,000 could drop a good deal without changing the fact that it's practically rational to choose theism. Pascal seems in fact to suggest, and others have concurred, that the value of an eternal reward is infinite instead of finite. It is difficult to know what an infinite utility is like. What's more, we're about to see an objection to Pascal's argument that raises a challenge for it no matter whether the utility of an eternal reward is finite or infinite. For these reasons, I'll continue to work with finite utilities.

What questions might we raise for Pascal? Let's not forget, first of all, about the *subjective* part of subjective expected utility: You are the one who needs to think about how much you'd value Heaven or disvalue Hell. For instance, while we might not be clear what Heaven would be like, a naïve conception of it as populated with angels flying around singing hymns might not appeal to you. You might ask: What would I find so great about that? Likewise, if you're not a theist, then eternal damnation might be a punishment that you find unfair. You might say, "If I'm not a theist because I haven't found enough evidence to believe in a GCB, and I die and go to Hell for this, then I know it will be unpleasant. But at least I'll have my self-respect with me. At least I'll be able to say that I stood up for what I believed (or didn't believe) in!" Someone who thinks this way might not find the prospect of Hell as terrible as do others. In that case her evaluation of the possible outcomes of her actions might not favor theism over nontheism.

Here are some other questions that can be raised for Pascal's line of reasoning. First is an objection that Pascal himself foresees. One might wonder how, even if we are convinced that it is practically rational to be a theist, one might come by belief in a GCB. After all, for the most part I cannot form beliefs at will. Even if someone offers me a large sum of money to do so, I cannot at will form the belief that I am made of glass, or that the Moon is made of cheese. So, too, with the existence of a GCB. Pascal acknowledges this problem and suggests that one can cultivate theism over time by doing such things as going to church regularly and surrounding oneself with believers. A contemporary version of this solution would have you do these things, and perhaps also hire a hypnotist or listen to lots of contemporary religious music, such as Christian rock. Pascal suggests that although the process may take years, after a while you stand a good chance of having faith come to "stupefy your scruples," to borrow William James' piquant phrase.

Pascal seems to be on strong ground in replying to this last objection. Another objection to Pascal goes like this. "If I become a theist on self-interested grounds such as those Pascal proposes, should a GCB really want to reward me? Following the suggestion of Pascal's argument seems to require that I be a theist simply out of selfish reasons." In reply, we might remark first of all that by the end of the belief-inducing process mentioned in the last paragraph, you will be just as devout a believer as anyone else. For the belief-inducement process to work, you must be unable to remember that you can't find arguments that make a persuasive case that theism is theoretically rational. (If you did remember, your theism would probably be undermined.) Presumably you will think there is some such sound argument, and that will make you sweat with conviction just as much as the next theist does. We might also bear in mind that many people come upon systems of belief or action in an originally self-interested way, but that fact does not undermine their current commitment or sincerity. For instance, we often get children to do what is right by a system of incentives, and when they follow those incentives they are behaving in their own self-interest. However, eventually many children start to follow morality not for the sake of self-interest but for the rightness of actions that morality enjoins. Citing such a child's wanton past does not undermine her current virtue.

Pascal seems to have successful replies to the two foregoing objections. It is less clear what he would have to say in reply to the following objection, which starts with a simple question from J. Cargile: "How do we know that the possible owner-operator of the universe is the sort of being who will send religious people to Heaven?"[4] That

[4] J. Cargile, "Pascal's Wager," *Philosophy*, vol. 41, pp. 250–57.

is, even granting that there is a non-zero chance of a GCB, or at least some Very Great Being existing, what reason do we have for thinking that that Being will reward all and only those people who are theists? After all, there's no obvious connection between such a Being existing and wanting people to worship Him or Her; further, even if that Being does enjoin worship, it is yet another step to the idea that all and only those who worship Him or Her are rewarded.

Accordingly, the above matrix needs to be formulated more carefully. Instead of two possible states of the world, we need to distinguish three, namely that in which the GCB exists and rewards theists with eternal bliss; that in which the GCB exists and sends all theists to eternal damnation; and that in which the GCB does not exist. Cargile suggests that we have no reason to think that the first two of these three possible states is more likely than the second. Suppose that each of these states has a 1 percent likelihood, and that the third has a 98 percent likelihood. You can work out for yourself a matrix showing how this newly recognized possibility balances out the earlier one in such a way that the expected utility of theism is now no higher than the expected utility of not being a theist. This last line of thought is called the "many Gods objection" to Pascal's wager and is a subject of controversy today.

The argument from morality

We have considered three attempts to show that theism is theoretically rational, and one attempt to show that theism is practically rational. None of these has turned out to be quite convincing on closer scrutiny. "Well," you might say, "All these arguments seem a *bit* persuasive; why not just argue for the existence of a GCB by putting them all together?"

This won't work. Soundness isn't a matter of degree—an argument is either sound or it is not. Ninety-nine intriguing but failed attempts to prove the existence of a square circle don't add up to a successful proof that such a thing exists. Similarly, lots of failed attempts to prove the existence of a GCB don't add up to a successful proof.

Instead, I'll attempt one more argument, one that challenges us to figure out where morality could have come from if not from a higher being such as the GCB. You've probably heard this line of reasoning in some form in the past. In fact, in the Introduction to this book we imagined some people discussing a movie over coffee, and one person urged, "If there's no God there's no morality either." That slogan is associated with the idea that the only possible source of morality would have to be a divine being. More precisely, it suggests that the only possible explanation of the existence of morality is that it was created by an intelligent, sentient creator, who is presumably benevolent as well as powerful enough to create morality.

This attempt to prove the existence of a GCB was discussed as far back as Plato. Quite possibly the most famous philosopher in Western history, Plato (c. 428–347 BCE) was a student of Socrates (469–399 BCE), who spent his adult life hanging around in Athens chatting with others about philosophy. Socrates was notorious for raising difficult questions about virtue, justice, and related notions, and he often showed others were mistaken in their confident views about these topics. Eventually Socrates irritated the other citizens of Athens so much that they tried him in court and put him to death. When young, Plato and other men followed Socrates around as much as possible listening to, and at times engaging in, his philosophical discussions. Plato wrote down some of these discussions, and his writings are among our most important historical sources about the character and views of Socrates.

Plato's dialogue *Euthyphro* is named after an Athenian citizen that, according to this dialogue, Socrates bumps into in front of the law courts. Socrates asks Euthyphro what brings him there, and his friend replies that he is there to prosecute his father for murder. Socrates is surprised that anyone would do such a thing and tells Euthyphro that he must be pretty confident that he knows what morality is if he is prosecuting his own father. Euthyphro replies to the effect, "You're darn right I do." Socrates then eagerly asks Euthyphro what morality is—a question Socrates has been trying to answer for years. Euthyphro replies that it is whatever is loved by the gods. (Remember that ancient Greece was polytheistic.)

Socrates now challenges Euthyphro's answer, which seems to say that it is the decree of God(s) that makes a given act right or wrong, as the case may be. On this approach, God decrees that murder shall be wrong, that keeping promises right, and so on. But let's pause for a moment and examine that alleged decree. We can imagine God going through all the possible actions—murder, promise-keeping, torturing innocent children, caring for those who can't help themselves—and deciding which ones go on the "right" pile, and which go on the "wrong" pile. (Many, like scratching one's elbow, may go on neither.) There seem to be two possibilities as to how God makes these decisions: Either the decisions are arbitrary, made with no reason at all; or they are not arbitrary, and so are made for a reason. Since the GCB is infallible, that reason must be one that truly justifies the choice, rather than one that merely seems to justify the choice but does not.

If the GCB's choice is arbitrary, then it can't be a decree of morality. Why not? Because an arbitrary decree, no matter whose decree it is, can't *make* an act right if it wasn't right already. An arbitrary decree might make driving on one, rather than the other, side of the road illegal; an arbitrary decree might also make eating with one's left hand socially improper. These, however, are matters of law or etiquette, not of morality. Again, someone or something might also decree that one must *call* a certain action right and another action wrong. That of course doesn't make that action wrong. Actions are right or wrong, it seems, regardless of what we call them. An arbitrary decree just doesn't seem like the kind of thing that could create morality.

Suppose, on the other hand, that the GCB's decree of morality, rather than being arbitrary, is based on reasons. In that case, the GCB *discerns* rather than stipulates those reasons. If the reasons for calling a given act right are ones that the GCB discerns, then those reasons are there independent of the GCB. For instance, the reason for calling murder wrong might be that persons have a right not to be deprived of their lives. The GCB doesn't bestow that right on anybody; people have it because they are people. If that is correct, though, then if the GCB's decree of morality is *justified,* it is no *decree* at all. The most it could be is a *realization* that some acts are right and others are wrong. Socrates, in espousing this reasoning, can accept that the omniscient GCB is the only being that can truly and infallibly know what morality is. However, that doesn't show that the GCB *makes* that morality to which it has infallible access. We can't, it seems, make good sense of the idea that the GCB makes morality, so the existence of morality is no evidence in favor of the GCB.

Atheological Arguments

We have considered five arguments that attempt to show that theism is rational; four of our arguments employ theoretical rationality, and one employs practical rationality. We found all of these arguments wanting, but if you think one or more of them can be strengthened, then I encourage you to try to do so.

I will now take up a famous line of thought that purports to show that belief in the GCB is positively irrational, namely the problem of evil. First, however, it will be useful to take a detour through a well-known paradox.

The paradox of the stone

It has been held that the very concept of the GCB is self-contradictory or at least incoherent. Let us leave that aside, however, and note that it is hard to see how the GCB could make a stone so heavy that it can't be moved—even by the GCB. On the one hand the GCB is usually thought to be omnipotent, and one might understand omnipotence as meaning that the GCB can do anything. But in that case the GCB ought to be able to make that immovable stone. However, if it does make an immoveable stone, then there will be something it cannot do, namely lift the stone that it has made. On the other hand, if the GCB can't make this stone and lift it, then there is also something that it cannot do. Hence in either case there is something that the GCB cannot do: If the GCB can make the stone, then there is something that it cannot do (lift it), and so it's not omnipotent after all; and if it can't make that stone, then it surely isn't omnipotent either.

Does this show that the very idea of a GCB is incoherent or self-contradictory? Perhaps not. Let's back up a moment to rethink the very notion of omnipotence. An offhand definition of omnipotence might be "being able to do anything." But if you reflect on this for a moment, it might not seem so clear that this definition is correct. After all, it is very hard to see what it could mean to say that an omnipotent being could make a four-sided circle. A figure with four sides wouldn't be a set of points on a plane equidistant from a single point on that same plane. It would seem instead that a four-sided circle is simply impossible. Does it count as an objection to a being's omnipotence that it can't do impossible things? It's difficult to see why. If you came across a person who doubted the GCB's omnipotence because that Being couldn't make a square circle, you might feel she was being unreasonable. It seems, in fact, much more reasonable to require that an omnipotent being be able to do *anything that it is possible to do.* If it is not possible to add three things to two other things and get six things, then that need not be an objection to a being's omnipotence as we have clarified the term.[5]

Suppose that, rather than construing omnipotence as the ability to do anything at all (even the impossible things), we construe omnipotence as the ability to do anything that it is possible to do. Then we can make some progress with our problem about the stone. For perhaps the lesson of this problem is that making an unliftable stone is simply not possible, any more than it is possible to count to the largest prime number or draw a square circle. That would be compatible with the GCB's being omnipotent, of course, on our current proposal. It would also provide a useful twist to Clint Eastwood's remark, "A man's gotta know his limitations." In the present context, the slogan would go something like, "Even an omnipotent being's gotta know Its limitations: It can only do what it's possible do to." (But you should still say this with a scowl.)

If we define omnipotence as "being able to do whatever it is possible to do," then our question about the unliftable stone won't call into doubt the coherence of the idea of a GCB. Perhaps one might call into doubt the GCB's existence on empirical rather than conceptual grounds. One famous attempt to do so is the problem of evil.

The problem of evil

The GCB is normally credited with responsibility for creating the world. But there certainly seems a lot of pain, suffering, wickedness, and malevolence in the world. Why then is not God responsible for all this misery? If there is some feasible way within my means of making the world better, I would like to think that I would take the opportunity to do so: If I could prevent wars, sickness, or other forms of suffering, I wouldn't hesitate to do so. My inability to do these things is due to limitations on my intelligence and power; I cannot claim that I am infinitely benevolent. However, a GCB is all of these things, so what gives?

In coming to grips with the problem, let us distinguish two kinds of evil, moral and physical. *Moral evil* is the intentional production of a harm or suffering by a free agent. Examples of moral evil include

[5] It won't help to say in reply that an omnipotent being could change the definition of "square" so that it applies to round things, or that it could change the definition of "two" so that it really means "three." Doing so would show nothing about squares or the number two. By the same token I hope you're not convinced by the following argument that capital punishment is morally wrong: (1) Capital punishment can be defined as "judicial murder." (2) Murder is morally wrong. Therefore, (3) capital punishment is morally wrong.

intentionally hurting someone by causing them pain; intentionally deceiving them for the purpose of taking advantage of them; or purposely making someone the object of ridicule. By contrast, *physical evil* is the production of a harm or suffering by something other than a free agent. Sudden Infant Death Syndrome, for instance, does not seem to be the result of anybody's intentional behavior, and yet it is a harm; diseases produce a great deal of physical evil, as do natural disasters such as tsunamis or hurricanes. There seems little doubt that the world is replete with instances of both physical and moral evil.

With the aid of these notions of moral and physical evil, a philosopher might expound an atheological argument:

1. Suppose that the GCB exists.
2. Being omnipotent, omniscient, and omnibenevolent, the GCB would prevent any evil—moral or physical—that could be prevented.
3. There exist many evils—both moral and physical—that could be prevented.
4. The GCB is either not omniscient, or not omnipotent, or not omnibenevolent.

ergo, 5. The GCB does not exist.

Here are some responses to the above line of reasoning.

"God is giving us a test"

It is sometimes said that in allowing us to engage in moral evil, or in allowing us to suffer, God is giving us a test. The test in question presumably determines whether we are qualified for an eternity in Heaven. A test might account for why God allows us to engage in wrongdoing, or to see how we respond to suffering either in ourselves or in others. This approach in effect denies premise 2 in the argument above. However, it does so at the expense of God's omniscience. After all, the great majority of theists also believe that God sees into our future; indeed if there is a real future to be seen into, then omniscience mandates that God be able to see it. So it would seem that if God is a GCB, the test results are already in; God would know even before we are born what we are going to do and how we will react to any suffering that might be meted out to us. It would, then, be simply perverse to say that God would allow moral or physical evil in order to carry out tests to which God knows the answers beforehand. This avenue of response thus does not seem promising.

"Evil is just a privation"

It is sometimes said that evil is a privation, just as shadow is the absence of light rather than a thing itself. Then, it might be added, while God is perhaps responsible for the real things and their characteristics, God is not responsible for the non-things. This response seems to be denying premise 3 of the above argument. However, I confess to not being sure that I understand this response; and I confess that insofar as I can make sense of it, it seems like a verbal subterfuge. Consider a case of evil: A child suffers horribly from a degenerative neurological disorder and dies before the age of four. I don't care whether you call it a privation or not or whether you compare it to a shadow—the fact is that it is a terrible thing. The question still arises, regardless of what you call this event, how could it be allowed by a GCB? You might reply, "Well, my point about privations and such is just that this event, just like a shadow, is not a thing at all." To this I would reply in return, "It sure *looks* like a thing, indeed a very terrible and tragic thing. A thing I wish hadn't happened. Try telling the child's parents that this wasn't an event at all, it was just a privation, a non-thing. I think they wouldn't understand you, and neither would I."

We may note as well that even if we grant that evil is a privation and thus in some sense not a thing at all, one can simply reformulate the problem of evil to accommodate this fact. The problem may now be formulated as the question, Why does God permit so many non-things? or, alternatively, Why does God bring about so few instances of good as compared to the number that could have been brought about? Surely the suffering child missed out on a life in which she might have loved or helped others, and if we choose to banish the mystery about this with the notion of a "privation," it will simply reappear in the form of a question about the *paucity* of good.

"Things balance out" (a.k.a. "ultimate harmony doctrine")

It is often suggested that for all that our finite and limited minds can discern, for each quantity of evil in the world, there might be a compensating quantity of good somewhere else in space or time, or even outside of space and time. The aforementioned child's death might allow her to spend that much more time in Heaven; evil now might afford me wisdom later; suffering in one place might create elsewhere a deeper appreciation of what is good. This suggestion might point us toward a plausible response to the problem of evil, and its gist is to deny premise 2 of our atheological argument. However, it lays itself open to the following challenge. As Nelson Pike points out in his article "Hume on Evil," this response suggests that God is like a husband who beats his wife one day only to make it up to her the next day with roses and chocolates.[6] Perhaps the husband does compensate for his earlier wrongs (though I tend to doubt it), but he certainly seems to be *inferior* to a husband who doesn't cause black eyes and broken ribs in the first place. Likewise, even if there is some good somewhere in the universe that balances out the evil elsewhere, the question is, of course, why does there have to be the evil in the first place? Why did God have to give us black eyes and broken ribs, either literally or metaphorically? We might put answers to this question under the banner:

"No mountains without valleys"

I would suggest that the first two responses to the problem of evil (The "God is giving us a test" view, and the "Evil is a privation" view) do not seem especially promising, and that what plausibility we may find in the third response (the ultimate harmony doctrine) is because it is yet another form of this fourth response. How does this response go? Just as there cannot be mountains without valleys, it might be said that so too there cannot be good without evil. If this is right, then at least some evil is justifiable, and cannot be used as evidence against the existence of a GCB. That is, in effect to deny premise 2 of our theological argument above, for it suggests that if the GCB were to prevent certain evils, something even greater would be lost.

As we consider this response more carefully, we'll need to keep two issues distinct:

(A) Is the existence of some evil compatible with the existence of a GCB?
(B) Is the existence of the actual amount of evil compatible with the existence of a GCB?

Let us use the term *defense* for any reasoning that (successfully) shows that the existence of a GCB is compatible with the existence of some evil. Such a defense would thus show that from the mere fact that some evil does exist, we cannot infer that the GCB does not. By contrast, let us use the term "theodicy" for any reasoning that (successfully) shows that the existence of a GCB is compatible with

[6] Nelson Pike, "Hume on Evil," *The Philosophical Review,* vol. 72 (1963): 180–97.

the actual amount of evil in the world. As we're about to see, a fairly strong case can be made in favor of an affirmative answer to (A)—that is, that a defense is possible. But even if this is so, that will not be enough to answer (B), or to provide a theodicy. The reason is, of course, that the actual world contains a lot more than just some evil; it contains a great deal. Further, from the fact that some evil is justifiable, it does not follow that the actual *amount* of evil is justifiable. Analogously, a factory may have no choice, given available technology and economic exigencies, other than to produce some pollution. However, that fact may not be enough to justify the amount of pollution the factory coughs out into the air.

Let us turn to an examination of (A). This may take either of two forms, depending on whether we are focusing on moral or on physical evil. Can the existence of some amount of physical evil be justified? Sure. It seems quite reasonable that in order to appreciate the pleasures associated with health, I should be acquainted with its occasional lapse. Illness every once in a while might make me better appreciate physical health when I am returned to it. Perhaps, too, a certain amount of pain is requisite in order for me to appreciate pleasure. Further, it might be held that God, seeing that a universe in which there is pleasure is better than a universe in which there is no pleasure at all, will permit some physical evil to exist as well in order to create this better universe. God is in this respect like the owner of the factory that pollutes; in this case a certain amount of physical evil is an unavoidable by-product of physical good. Notice that we can agree to these suggestions without agreeing to the much stronger claims that the actual amount of physical evil is justified.

What about moral evil? Can some amount of moral evil be justified? It seems pretty clear that it can. As before, God may have seen that a world in which there is some moral good is better than a world in which there is no moral good. A world, for instance, in which the highest living things are goldfish seems impoverished. To the best of our knowledge, goldfish lack moral attributes: They can't tell the truth, keep promises, respect one another, return favors, extend forgiveness, and so forth. But, we might point out, these moral attributes are wonderful things. They enrich a world; some might even say that they make our lives worth living. However, for such attributes to occur they must occur in agents who are free. Creatures unable to make choices between right and wrong, in particular, don't have any moral attributes. As a result, God would quite reasonably create free agents able to choose between right and wrong. However, God has no choice but to take the good with the bad. Where there is freedom there is also the possibility of moral wrongdoing, and, alas, moral wrongdoing is sometimes found. However, a world in which there is some moral evil is justifiable because it is a world in which there is also moral good.

We may agree that where there is moral good there is also the possibility of moral evil. However, it doesn't follow that the latter possibility has to be actualized. Consider all the possible free agents that God might have created. Presumably there are either infinitely many or a *very* large number of them. God, being omniscient, knows beforehand what all these agents are going to do even before they are brought into existence (if they are). God therefore also knows who, among all the possible free agents, are always going to freely choose what is right. These are what we might call *moral saints*. Surely such moral saints are possible? And if they are, why didn't God choose to create only them? J. L. Mackie makes just this point when he asks in his article "Evil and Omnipotence":[7]

> "If God has made men such that in their free choices they sometimes prefer what is good and sometimes what is evil, why could he not have made men such that they always freely choose the good?"

Of all the possible free agents, why could not God have created only those whom God knew beforehand would choose only to do what is right? (Granted, I would not have been brought into existence, but perhaps I didn't deserve to be!) A reply immediately suggests itself, namely, that such people, if created by God, would not really be free after all. The thought behind this reply is that, if any one of them *had* chosen to do what is wrong, she would never have been allowed to exist.

Mackie will not take this lying down. I imagine he might offer us an analogy. Consider a body authorized to appoint a new president of a corporation. This body might agree that they should only appoint a person who, they are confident, is of impeccable integrity. They narrow the field down from one hundred candidates to just one, Susan, of whose integrity they are as confident as they can imagine being. Now when they appoint her, the body of electors feels confident that she will always do what is right. But surely this does not mean that Susan

[7] "Evil and Omnipotence," *Mind,* vol. 64 (1955): 200–212.

is not free. After her appointment, on any given day as president of the corporation, she might do wrong. We just know that she won't.

So far we don't have a strong reason for believing that wherever there is moral good there must also be some moral evil. However, it does seem that some moral virtues require the existence of moral evil. I cannot *forgive* someone, it seems, unless they have wronged me. But their wronging me would appear to be nothing other than a case of moral evil. Physical evil might be required for the realization of such virtues as compassion. I cannot feel compassion for someone who is not suffering in some way. Courage is also a virtue, but it can't be realized in a world in which there are no challenges, and likewise for other virtues.

Suppose now that we have been convinced that the realization of certain moral qualities requires the existence of some physical evil, some moral evil, or both. That would be enough to give us a defense. Yet in so doing it doesn't give us a theodicy. If one is to respond to the atheological argument, you'll need to give some reason for thinking that such a theodicy is possible.

Here is one attempt to go beyond a mere defense without quite going so far as to aim for a theodicy. Robert Adams, in his article, "Must God Create the Best?"[8] challenges the assumption that if God creates any world at all, it must be the very best world that God can create. In light of what we've just said about virtues like forgiveness and compassion, the very best possible world might still contain some evil, but it would contain no more evil than is absolutely necessary for these moral virtues. Adams also asks us to assume for simplicity that there is such a thing as the very best possible world. Accordingly, we will leave aside the question whether possible worlds might improve in quality in the same way that integers increase in size.

Adams asks us to imagine a situation in which God creates a world that is less good than might have been created. He asks us to assume a world that meets three conditions: (1) Assume that in such a world, no creature in it also exists in the best of all possible worlds; (2) assume further that in such a world, no creature's life is so miserable that it would have been better off not existing at all; and finally, (3) assume that no creature in this world would have been better off in any other possible world in which it might have existed. Adams then asks us what would be morally objectionable about a world meeting these three conditions. If God has done wrong in creating such a world, then it is either because God

[8] "Must God Create the Best?" *The Philosophical Review,* vol. 81 (1972): 317–32.

has wronged some creature in creating that world or because God has shown some kind of moral perversity in creating such a world without necessarily wronging anyone.

God hasn't wronged any creature in creating the world in question, Adams argues. He assumes first of all that the only creatures that can be wronged are actual creatures rather than merely possible creatures. As a result, no actual creature can complain about not being created in the best possible world, for it wouldn't have existed there. Further, the possible creatures that exist in the best possible world haven't been wronged because they are merely possible; none of them is actual.

Adams also argues that in creating the envisioned world, God hasn't shown any kind of moral perversity. One might show moral perversity without harming anyone by, for instance, attempting to do harm but failing. If I fire a gun at someone I despise but the bullet misses and no harm is done, I've still shown moral perversity, even if no one is harmed. Adams argues that in the case of the world he envisions, God will be sure to love all existing creatures fully. Accordingly, this makes it hard to see how God could really be perverse in creating this admittedly suboptimal world.

What if someone objects: "Hey, you might as well say that it would be perfectly fine if a mother who has a deep interest in special needs children takes a pill resulting in her child's being born with a serious birth defect. Even if she unstintingly devotes her life to the well-being of the child, she has still done something wrong in taking that pill. Isn't that like God choosing to create a less excellent world than He might have created?"

Adams sees the force of this response but suggests a rejoinder in turn. He tells us that it's immoral for the mother to take this pill. Her taking it shows, at the very least, a moral perversity, because she does something to make the child exist at a level that is substandard relative to what is normal for human beings. By contrast, God's creating the world we have imagined does not require doing any such thing. Consider an analogy. A man chooses to breed goldfish rather than puppies. Puppies are a lot more interesting than goldfish; they have a greater capacity for learning, emotions, and fun than goldfish do. However, intuitively it seems that if someone chooses to breed goldfish rather than puppies, then so long as he takes good care of the goldfish and gives them lives that are normal for what can be expected of animals of that kind, he has done nothing wrong. Adams will suggest that God, in creating a world that is not the best of all possible worlds, but is still a world that meets the conditions specified above, is like the man who breeds goldfish rather than puppies. God *might* have created a better world, but the fact that God didn't shows neither that anyone has been wronged nor any moral perversity. This, at least, is the case so long as the lives of the creatures in this world are normal relative to what can be expected of their species.

I said that Adams does not attempt to give a theodicy by means of the argument I have just discussed. However, Adams is giving more than a defense, because he is arguing that the existence of some unnecessary evil is compatible with the existence and attributes of a GCB. Can Adams' argument be turned into a theodicy? In order to do this, we would have to argue that the actual world, the one we in fact live in, meets the three criteria that Adams lays down. Is it, however, true, that no creature in this world is so badly off that it would have been better if it had not existed at all? There surely seem to be a lot of creatures in this world that live lives at levels seriously below what seems normal relative to their species! Ask yourself whether the actual world meets Adams' three conditions. In so doing you may see not only the value of Adams' contribution but also the distance that would have to be traveled before we would have a genuine theodicy in our hands.

We began this chapter with the question whether belief concerning the existence or nonexistence of a GCB can be justified on theoretical, pragmatic, or moral grounds. We found that arguments justifying theism are tantalizing but not fully compelling. We then turned to atheological arguments and found that while the paradox of the stone does not seem to show that the idea of a GCB is incoherent, the problem of evil does raise a real challenge for theism. However, perhaps that challenge can be met by building on ideas such as those of Adams. More generally, rather than seeing the inconclusive nature of the arguments we've considered so far to show that agnosticism is the only reasonable position to hold on the existence of the GCB, another and more satisfying response would be to see our work so far as an invitation, or even a provocation, to develop one or more of the above lines of reasoning more fully. Recalling my suggestion in Chapter 1 that philosophy is more a skill than an established body of knowledge, if you have strong feelings about the existence of a GCB, I hope you will see this chapter as preparing you to refine and develop your own thinking on this question.

Study Questions

1. William Paley's argument from design tries to justify theism by means of an analogy with a very special, imaginary watch. Please explain the most important features of this analogy. On the basis of this analogy, Paley contends that the only way to account for the apparent complexity and design observable in the world is by postulating an intelligent, sentient designer. How might Charles Darwin's theory of evolution by natural selection pose a challenge to Paley's contention? Must we accept Darwin's theory as definitely true in order to pose a challenge to Paley's argument? Please explain your answer.

2. Aquinas, in his "The Five Ways," holds that a chain of causes cannot stretch back infinitely. If we accept Aquinas' assumption, is it possible to infer the existence of a GCB? Please explain your answer.

3. Samuel Clarke's cosmological argument distinguishes between dependent and independent beings. Please explain this distinction. Clarke's argument for a GCB is important because it does not assume, as Aquinas does, that there cannot be an infinite causal regression of dependent beings. How does Clarke argue that even if there is an infinite causal regression of dependent beings, there must also be at least one independent being?

4. Anselm tries to prove the existence of a GCB just by referring both to its very definition and to the concept of existence. Please explain this line of reasoning. The monk Gaunilo counters that if Anselm's argument were sound, it would also prove something absurd, such as the existence of the Greatest Conceivable Island. Please explain Gaunilo's point. Finally, how does Anselm withstand Gaunilo's objection by pointing out a crucial difference between a GCB and a GCI?

5. Pascal argues that even if it not theoretically rational to believe in a GCB, it is nevertheless practically rational to do so. After briefly explaining the act/state/outcome approach to practical rationality, show how Pascal arrives at this conclusion. Does the success of Pascal's argument depend on how much an individual values the "eternal reward," such as that promised in Heaven? Please explain your answer.

6. Pascal argues that even if it is not theoretically rational to believe in a GCB, it is nevertheless practically rational to do so. Suppose that he can argue persuasively for this conclusion. It still seems difficult to form a belief at will just because I deem it prudential to do so. How might Pascal suggest that we overcome this difficulty? Also, one might object to Pascal's wager by suggesting that a GCB would not reward a person who becomes a theist on the basis of apparently crass prudential considerations such as those offered by the wager argument. How might Pascal respond to this objection?

7. In his response to Pascal's wager, Cargile asks ("Pascal's Wager"), "How do we know that the possible owner-operator of the universe is the sort of being who will send religious people to Heaven?" (p. 253) If we think through the significance of this question, we may see that it poses a challenge to the cogency of Pascal's argument for the practical rationality of theism. Please explain why this is so.

8. Please explain the difference between *moral evil* and *physical evil*. Next, explain why it might be thought that the existence of either form of evil supports an atheological argument. Finally, why might it be held that in order to realize a world in which many moral virtues are found, there must also be some moral evil as well as some physical evil?

9. Here are four slogans that might be invoked to respond to the atheological argument from evil. Please briefly explain each of these slogans, and explain whether it offers a plausible response to that atheological argument: (1) "God is giving us a test"; (2) "Evil is just a privation"; (3) "Things balance out"; (4) "No mountains without valleys."

10. Please explain the difference between a *defense* and a *theodicy* as these words are used in the context of the problem of evil. In light of this distinction, explain the salient features of Adams' argument in his "Must God Create the Best?" that a GCB need not create the best of all possible worlds. (In your answer it may be helpful to recall Adams' example of the person who chooses to breed goldfish rather than puppies, as well as his example of the mother who takes a drug causing a deformity in her unborn fetus, but who loves it unstintingly after it is born.) Can Adams' position plausibly be seen as offering a theodicy, and not merely a defense? Please explain your answer.

Suggestions for Further Reading

An accessible introduction to a number of core texts by Charles Darwin is *Charles Darwin on Evolution: The Development of the Theory of Natural Selection,* edited by T. Glick and D. Kohn. Indianapolis: Hackett Publishing Company, 1996.

A detailed yet eminently accessible discussion of the theory of evolution by natural selection is Richard Dawkins, *Climbing Mount Improbable.* New York: Norton, 1998. Dawkins pays particular attention to assessing modern forms of the argument from design. Recently a number of writers have defended the doctrine of intelligent design, which accepts many of the claims of evolution by natural selection while denying that ENS can account for all the apparent complexity and design that we find in the organic world. For a discussion of this movement see H. Allen Orr, "Devolution: Why Intelligent Design Isn't." *The New Yorker,* May, 2005. Available online at www.newyorker.com.

An introduction to the writings of Aquinas may be found in *Thomas Aquinas: On Faith and Reason,* edited by Stephen F. Brown. Indianapolis: Hackett Publishing Company, 1999.

One of the West's greatest works in the philosophy of religion is *Hume's Dialogues Concerning Natural Religion,* 2nd edition, edited by Richard Popkin. Indianapolis: Hackett Publishing Company, 1998.

Anselm's ontological argument, as well as his exchange with Gaunilo, may be found in his *Proslogion,* translated by T. Williams. Indianapolis: Hackett Publishing Company, 2001.

Pascal's famous "wager" argument may be found in his *Pensées,* translated by Roger Ariew. Indianapolis: Hackett Publishing Company, 2005.

Plato's dialogue *Euthyphro* may be found in *Five Dialogues,* 2nd edition, translated by G. Grube and J. Cooper. Indianapolis: Hackett Publishing Company, 2002.

A wide-ranging anthology containing many of the central texts of the philosophy of religion is *God,* 2nd edition, edited by T. Robinson. Indianapolis: Hackett Publishing Company, 2003. See also John Perry's *A Dialogue on Good, Evil, and the Existence of God.* Indianapolis: Hackett Publishing Company, 1999.

Richard Swinburne in *The Existence of God,* 2nd edition. Oxford: Oxford University Press, 2004, develops the "cumulative case" argument for theism.

A profound meditation on the nature of moral evil (his own) may be found in Saint Augustine's *Confessions,* translated by F. Sheed. Indianapolis: Hackett Publishing Company, 1993.

A text treating the philosophy of religion at a more advanced level is K. Yandell, *The Philosophy of Religion.* London: Routledge, 1999.

Movies Significant for the Philosophy of Religion

Wings of Desire (1987), directed by Wim Wenders.

The Rapture (1991), directed by Michael Tolkin.

4. Right and Wrong

In our last chapter we found ourselves contemplating the nature and extent of evil in the world. Our definition of moral evil presupposed that we know what it means for an act to be wrong or, by contrast, what it means for an act to be right. However, we might very well wonder what these things mean, and when we pursue this question self-consciously we are engaging with the field of ethics. In this chapter we'll consider some of the central questions that ethicists raise as well as some of the most important answers that have been proffered to those questions.

I take the most central question in ethics to be: What makes right acts right? It is easy to see how this question also leads to the related question, what makes wrong acts wrong? We will be considering a number of important answers to these questions, paying attention to their historical sources where it's relevant.

Ethical Egoism

A straightforward and bracing answer to the question, What makes right acts right?, is whatever is in my own best interests. We already have a framework, in the doctrine of subjective expected utility, for explicating that position. The *ethical egoist,* that is, tells us that the right act is whatever maximizes his own subjective expected utility. You can be an egoist in this sense without being an "egotist" as that word is used in everyday parlance, where it means, "conceited, boastful person." You can be an ethical egoist without boasting or thinking yourself better than others. Similarly, although I'm using the expression "ethical egoist" in part because it's pretty standard in the literature, one's being an ethical egoist doesn't by definition make one ethical! Instead, "ethical egoist" means "egoist about ethical questions."

According to our definition, one can also be an ethical egoist while still caring about other people's well-being. For example, if I am an ethical egoist and my happiness depends intimately upon the well-being of my daughter, then what is right for me depends at least in part upon what is good for her. For this reason I might value an outcome at least in part because it gives pleasure to my daughter. However, if an outcome produces happiness for someone about whose well-being I am indifferent, even a great deal of happiness, that outcome will have no moral significance for me if I am an ethical egoist.

Ethical egoism is a relatively simple theory, and it is not difficult to find people who are ethical egoists in the sense of that term being used here. Similarly, I'll bet you can think of a good number of familiar characters from novels or movies who would be ethical egoists as we are using this term. (Gordon Gecko from the movie *Wall Street,* and Judah from the movie *Crimes and Misdemeanors* are examples.) However, while a person might adhere to ethical egoism without committing a gross violation of theoretical or practical rationality, the view flies in the face of common sense. Most people who are not sociopaths would admit that there are many things that might be in their best interest but would nevertheless be wrong. For instance, I might devise a scheme to bilk thousands of elderly people out of their retirement savings. Suppose I act on this scheme and it works beautifully, making me fabulously wealthy while pushing these elderly people into squalor. So long as I am indifferent to the plight of these folks, ethical egoism tells us that I have done the right thing. That seems absurd. While I have served my own best interests, I seem to have done something terribly wrong. It seems, instead, as if the ethical egoist has gone from the premise that (a) bilking the older folks is best for me, to the conclusion that (b) bilking the older folks is right. That does not follow, and in fact the conclusion of this argument runs counter to common sense.

Admittedly, common sense is fallible: It was once common sense that the Earth is the center of the universe, and it was once common sense that disease is caused by witchcraft and sorcery. We now know that these views were incorrect. In fact, educated people now generally reject many views that were once thought to be common sense. However, the fact that a theory violates common sense is a *presumption* against it. Copernicus, for instance, had to overcome a very strong presumption against his heliocentric theory of the cosmos before getting people to give up the eminently sensible idea that the Earth is the center of the universe. (After all, it *feels* as if the Earth is the center of the universe.) I know of no clear evidence, intuitive, empirical, or otherwise, in favor of ethical egoism that suggests that we should look past its counterintuitive implications. For this reason we do well to consider ethical theories that might better square with common sense.

Utilitarianism

In the latter part of the 18th and early part of the 19th centuries philosophers vigorously began to formulate a moral doctrine that we can best understand by contrasting it with ethical egoism. According to the doctrine of utilitarianism, that act is right which, from among all those available, is most likely to produce the greatest overall amount of happiness. Another way of formulating this is saying that one is to perform that action which has the greatest subjective expected utility so long as utility is calculated in terms of the overall production of happiness, regardless of whose happiness it is. Thus, for instance, if I am to choose between two acts, one of which is certain to produce moderate happiness for me and no happiness for anyone else while the other of which is certain to produce slight happiness for one thousand people and none for me, utilitarianism tells us that it is right to choose the latter action. Utilitarianism thus tells us to maximize subjective expected utility, but to make sure that the outcomes are evaluated not in terms of how much *I* value them, but in how much value they produce for people generally.[1]

Proponents of utilitarianism are eager to remind us that individuals are not the only ones who perform actions. Insofar as corporations, governments, and other institutions can enact measures that have consequences for the well-being of society, utilitarianism applies to those measures as well. This seems perfectly reasonable: If your aim is the maximization of the overall amount of happiness, there can be no objection to asking large institutions to think in these terms as well. It is no accident that utilitarian philosophers have often campaigned on behalf of social reform when not writing their books.

Utilitarianism also has a democratic feel to it. My happiness is no more important than yours, and our happiness can in turn be outweighed by the needs of suffering millions across the globe. In addition, nothing in the utilitarian doctrine says that it only applies to

[1] One sometimes hears "The greatest good for the greatest number" as a description of utilitarianism. However, this is misleading inasmuch as it suggests that the theory is committed in principle to spreading happiness among as many people as possible. We will see in a moment that utilitarianism is committed to no such thing.

members of our own species. Gorillas, cats, and mice can feel pleasure and pain just as we can, and so it would seem, before we can justify liquidating lab animals in search of an appealing fragrance, we need to consider how much suffering we will cause on behalf of human olfactory pleasure. As we'll see in a moment, however, this democratic flavor of the theory runs risk of a tyranny of the majority. Before getting to that point, however, we need to clarify utilitarianism a bit further.

The English philosopher and social reformer Jeremy Bentham (1748–1832) propounded an early version of utilitarianism in which various forms of pleasure or happiness differ from one another only as a matter of degree. He defines "utility" as follows:

> By utility is meant that property in any object, whereby it tends to produce benefit, advantage, pleasure, good, or happiness (all this in the present case comes to the same thing).[2]

Bentham here seems to be telling us that different forms of happiness are like different units of money. For instance, you might feel that playing a good game of chess is a "higher" pleasure than is chewing a piece of bubble gum. Bentham might agree with you but would hold that each activity has a certain finite value, a certain amount of "utility," and that enough of one can be equal to the utility of the other. Thus on this view, at least if spread out over a long enough time, enough bubble-gum pleasures will add up to the pleasure of the good game of chess.

That seems questionable. I have nothing against bubble gum. I do, however, doubt that the experience of even a huge number of pieces can add up to the sort of pleasure I get from a good game of chess, from spiritual or emotional intimacy with someone I care for, from experience of a new culture, or from appreciation of a great novel. The bubble gum, even a huge number of pieces of bubble gum, just doesn't seem to be on the same level as these other things. Might we clarify utilitarianism so that it accommodates this observation?

James Mill was a friend of Jeremy Bentham, and James' son John Stuart was a prodigy. In his autobiography, for instance, John says he recalls starting to learn Greek at age 3! Among the many other things that John learned as a child was Bentham's utilitarianism, and he reflected carefully upon how the theory might be improved. In John

[2] From John Troyer's *The Classical Utilitarians: Bentham and Mill.* Indianapolis: Hackett Publishing Company, 2003.

Stuart Mill's classic work, *Utilitarianism,* he not only does just this but also offers other refinements and improvements upon Bentham's way of thinking. Mill (hereafter I will refer to John Stuart Mill as "Mill") suggests that some pleasures are "higher" than others, and then goes on to say what he means by that. First some examples: Stroking a piece of velvet is pleasant. So is soaking in a hot tub. I personally find going for a long run on a crisp fall day more pleasant than either of these things; you can think of various pleasures that you might rank as well, and your ranking might be different from mine. However, Mill suggests that in addition to the pleasures that are more or less bodily, many pleasures of an artistic, moral, or spiritual sort seem to be more valuable than any of the three that I just mentioned. For instance, the pleasure of appreciating a great work of literature is considerable and seems worth more than any of my three. Perhaps the same may be said for my appreciation of an outstanding piece of music. Your examples of higher pleasures might include falling in love, glimpsing the vastness of the universe, and learning some truths about the human condition.

Mill proposes that it is perfectly compatible with utilitarianism that some pleasures are "higher" than others, so that if pleasure P_1 is in the relevant sense higher than P_2, then an interval of experiencing P_1 is worth more utility than the same interval of P_2. Not only that, but in contrast to Bentham's thinking, the idea of being "worth more" can't always be cashed out along a single dimension of measurement. The pleasure of great literature is higher than that of bubble gum, but that doesn't mean that enough bubble-gum pleasure, even a great deal of it, adds up in such a way as to be equal to that of literary pleasure. Rather than using a numerical scale to measure the relative worth of pleasures, you might think of a lattice structure, where a pleasure's being "higher up" on the lattice than another means that the former is a higher pleasure, but nothing in the scheme tells you how much higher it is.

How do we figure out which pleasures are worth more than others, though? Mill's answer is pretty straightforward:

> Of two pleasures, if there be one to which all or almost all who have experience of both give a decided preference, irrespective of any feeling of moral obligation to prefer it, that is the more desirable pleasure. (*Utilitarianism*, p. 8)

Make sure that all the judges in question have experienced both P_1 and P_2, and make sure that they don't feel any moral obligation to prefer one over the other. For instance, as a teenager I listened to a lot of heavy metal, but very little jazz, classical, or other forms of music. For that reason, my conviction at age sixteen that certain musicians were the absolute pinnacles of musical greatness didn't count for much; I hadn't yet learned to appreciate the virtues of other musical genres or even other musicians within the genre of rock and roll. This suggests that a judge who is competent to compare two pleasures needs to be conversant with both. Similarly, a competent judge must have no moral convictions that bias their judgment about two kinds of pleasure. For instance, if they feel that classical music is elitist, then even if they are correct in this opinion, they are not very likely to appreciate the kind of pleasure it tries to provide. For that reason they will not be competent to judge the relative merits of classical music as compared to jazz, rock, soul, or bluegrass.

Assume then that we have a large group of judges possessed of a wide range of experience—for instance, they have a lot of experience listening to bluegrass music. Suppose further that they are free of any feeling of moral obligation to prefer one artist to any other, and suppose likewise that they don't prefer any one artist to another because of personal reasons. (For instance, they don't prefer one artist because he's their uncle.) Now, have a large number of judges experienced with both pleasures tell us which of these two they prefer. If all or most prefer P_1 over P_2, then according to Mill's test, P_1 is a higher pleasure than P_2. I believe that Mill would here go so far as to say that no other method even makes sense. After all, the quality of an experience is a matter of how much we like it. What could possibly show how much we like something other than the fact that most impartial people go for it?

One more clarification about the comparison of pleasures: Mill remarks that if, by his method, P_1 is judged higher than P_2, that need not be because P_1 is likely to produce a larger amount of pleasure than P_2 in the long run. That may be the case, but doesn't have to be. Instead, the difference in quality of pleasures is due to some inherent difference between them. Consider this case. Your cheapest supermarket cheese sold in a two-pound hunk is okay, but its flavor is neither complex nor subtle. On the other hand a piece of cheese sold in a gourmet shop, like an excellent Asiago or Brie, has subtle flavors that relate to one another in satisfying ways. Both cheeses will be equally filling, and let's suppose for simplicity that both have the same amount of fat, protein, and other nutritional values. In spite of these similarities, a Gorgonzola still produces a higher pleasure than the hunk of supermarket cheddar, and I feel confident that most competent judges would agree. Pleasures can be ranked, then, without reference to their consequences.

We might wonder whether utilitarianism sets too high a standard for the person trying to do what is right. It seems that to be a utilitarian I have to be on the "utility squad," ready to go produce happiness or minimize suffering wherever I am needed. If the Darfur region of the Sudan contains a lot of suffering refugees, then perhaps I should go there; or if I am needed to help respond to an earthquake in Ecuador, I should catch the next flight there. However, that lifestyle only suits some people. You might be different, but I would probably feel severe isolation after a few years of constantly being on the move from one hot spot to another. I am much happier having a degree of consistency in my life, not only in how I spend my time, but also in whom I see. It would be very hard for both me and my family, for instance, were I on the utility squad.

Mill acknowledges this concern and offers a useful response. Different people have different personalities. Some like consistency; others thrive on the excitement of responding to the latest crisis or challenge. These latter personalities are found in professions like emergency medicine, fire and rescue, and the police. They are exactly the sorts of people who would be good candidates for the "utility squad." Others, who like a degree of consistency and predictability in their lives, can be expected to produce happiness not by responding to each new crisis as it arises, but rather by producing things of value that require a long-term commitment: raising or teaching children, writing novels, finding cures for diseases, growing crops, or designing computers. If these latter people can also give to charity or give one weekend a year helping to build a house for someone less fortunate than themselves, then so much the better. Nevertheless, a society can be utilitarian even if only a small minority is charged with responding to emergencies. If most people do whatever they are best at, then so long as that activity or profession is not positively detrimental to the greater good they should keep doing what they've always been doing.

That is the "*too-high a standard*" objection, and Mill seems to have an adequate reply to it. Here is another objection: It might be pointed out that when we make a decision with potentially moral significance, we don't always have time to calculate which action has the highest subjective expected utility. There I am watching a child about to get hit by a bus. My instinct is to try to whisk him out of harm's way. However, to be a utilitarian, do I need to stop and calculate the expected utility of doing so? After all, maybe the child will grow up to be a criminal. Further, if the child's death is publicized widely, perhaps pedestrians and bus drivers will be more careful in the future. Does this show that utilitarianism is an unrealistic theory that expects us to write up a decision matrix every time we act? Let's call this the "*no time to calculate*" objection. As was the case with the "too-high a standard" objection, Mill has a useful reply to this objection too:

> The answer to the objection is that there has been ample time, namely, the whole past duration of the human species. (*Utilitarianism*, p. 23)

For consider a number of precepts that we learn from our parents and teachers:

Keep your promises.
Tell the truth.
Today is the first day of the rest of your life.
Many hands make light work.
To err is human, to forgive divine.
Do unto others as you would have them do unto you.
Two wrongs don't make a right.
Don't look a gift horse in the mouth.
To thine own self be true.

Many of these precepts have been part of the common heritage of at least the English-speaking world for generations and, in some cases, for centuries. Most of us have heard them so often they seem banal. Mill calls these "intermediate generalizations"; he suggests that these and hundreds of other precepts guide our moral decision making on an everyday basis, and, because of their familiarity, they do so in a way that is second nature to us. When someone asks you the time, you in most cases don't need to reflect on whether you should tell the truth; you just do. Likewise, when someone gives you a gift, you generally don't consider whether to "look it in the mouth," that is, to see whether its quality is up to your standards; you just accept it graciously. These precepts and others like them, Mill contends, guide our lives and make them go smoothly. It's a good thing, from a utilitarian point of view, that we try to be true to ourselves, keep our promises, tell the truth, and forgive others their errors. Life would probably be a lot worse if it we did not abide by these precepts.

Mill's point, then, is that in the great majority of cases you can be a good utilitarian by merely following the precepts that are part of our religious and moral heritage. Because these precepts are second nature for most of us, you can follow them without performing a utilitarian calculation every time you make a choice. (In fact, a little reflection shows that if you had to make a calculation every time you are deciding what to do, you'd never do anything, for then you'd have to decide whether to calculate what to do, and so on, forever.)

Mill seems to have reasonable replies to the "too-high a standard" and "no time to calculate" objections. However, it might now begin to look as if one can be a utilitarian without really trying. Does the theory have any bite at all, resulting in our doing anything different from what we normally do? Mill's answer is that it very probably does. Sometimes we will be faced with situations to which none of our intermediate generalizations applies. It surely isn't obvious that our religious and cultural heritage gives any particular guidance on ethical issues involving genetic engineering or free speech in the age of the Internet. Furthermore, in some cases our intermediate generalizations will give conflicting prescriptions. I might promise to protect you from harm if you are very vulnerable and you need my help. Yet what if the most feasible way to protect you is to tell a lie? Does that make the lie morally justified? Mill's answer is that the only way to settle the matter is to appeal to the principle of utility itself. If telling the lie will produce an overall balance of happiness over unhappiness, then tell the lie; otherwise, don't.

Suppose then that you're on your deathbed, due to no fault of mine, and I'm doing my best to comfort you. You only have a few hours to live, and you are very concerned about an overdue library book. You had asked me to return it yesterday, and I forgot. You now ask me whether I did return that book. It's clear that, given how you feel about overdue library books, your last few hours will be spent much less pleasantly if you think I did not return the book. What should I do? I hope that it's fairly clear that it would be reasonable for me to lie about the book. Here is a case in which intermediate generalizations conflict, but in which that conflict can be adjudicated by appealing to the overarching principle of maximizing expected utility. I would suggest also that it is no objection to utilitarianism that sometimes one does need to look beyond intermediate generalizations and think carefully about what to do.

Critiques of Utilitarianism

I hope you'll agree that utilitarianism has some virtues as an answer to the question, What makes right acts right? It seems hard to deny that morality has something to do with happiness, and Mill seems to have quite reasonable answers to the challenges that we have considered thus far. I now turn to some objections that Mill and those who follow him should find more troubling. First of all, observe that one problem with his method is that it's hostage to whoever happens to exist at a given time. Imagine that a fascist society manages to eradicate all opposition on the face of the Earth while instilling in its members the value of cruelty toward those born with congenital defects. In such a world most or all judges familiar with both experiences will prefer torturing children with Down's syndrome over eating a ham sandwich. That doesn't seem to show that the one activity is a higher pleasure than the other.

Further, one might doubt whether utilitarianism gives the right advice when rights and justice collide with considerations of utility. The doubt might begin to stir after we read Mill's remark, late in his *Utilitarianism,* suggesting that rights are dispensable:

> All persons are deemed to have a *right* to equality of treatment, except when some recognized social expediency requires the reverse. (*Utilitarianism*, p. 63)

This is a bit chilling. You have a right to being treated equally except when it is socially expedient not to recognize that right, and presumably Mill means utility maximization to be the arbiter of social expediency. Does that mean that the utilitarian society will recognize your right to be treated as autonomous unless expediency deems otherwise? Later on the same page Mill writes:

> . . . justice is a name for certain moral requirements which, regarded collectively, stand higher in the scale of social utility, and are therefore of more paramount obligation, than any others, though particular cases may occur in which some other social duty is so important as to overrule any one of the general maxims of justice. (Ibid.)

This might refer to cases in which governments curtail various civil liberties during times of crisis, such as war or social upheaval. Those measures might be justified. On the other hand, Mill might mean something more troubling, and to explain why, I shall argue that utilitarianism can justify doing things that seem, according to our ordinary moral beliefs, atrocious.

Consider this case. Rufus is a vagrant, hanging outside the local university hospital. He is apparently friendless and doesn't have much future as a contributing member of society. It is clear to the few that have paid him any attention that he wouldn't be much missed if he were suddenly to disappear. Dr. Jones is one of those few who have noticed this fact, and he reflects on it while thinking of how to save the lives of ten children, each of whom is a patient of his and each of whom is mortally ill. Dr. Jones feels unusually strongly about saving these ten lives, because these children all happen to be prodigies: one is a musical genius at age ten; another, a mathematical genius at age nine; a third has single-handedly created a charity for the underprivileged, and so forth. It is heartbreaking to think how much society will lose if these children perish. If only Dr. Jones could get kidneys for one, a heart for another, bone marrow for another, and so on!

Now it dawns on Dr. Jones: If he could harvest the organs of Rufus, he might be able to save those lives. He accordingly brings Rufus into his clinic for some routine medical treatment and makes a point of testing him to see whether as a donor he would be compatible with the kids who might benefit from his organs. He is—in fact, wonderfully so. Alone with his patient, Dr. Jones now arranges to anesthetize Rufus, and once Rufus is out cold Dr. Jones increases the level of anesthetic so that Rufus perishes. Now he calls in nurses and other practitioners, announcing that their patient has unexpectedly died on the hospital bed. Producing Rufus' organ donor card from his wallet, Dr. Jones next gives orders to have Rufus' organs and bone marrow harvested immediately and to begin the transplants and other operations that might save those ten children.

Has Dr. Jones done something that is right? I suppose most people would say no. We may even leave aside the Hippocratic oath,[3] which requires a physician to exercise his or her art solely for the cure of patients. Over and above the fact that Dr. Jones has not acted solely for the cure of his patient Rufus and so has violated the Hippocratic oath, he seems to have done something immoral, in spite of the fact that he seems to have done what utilitarianism would enjoin. For while Rufus was not likely to produce much happiness in the period of time remaining to him, enabling those ten kids to live is very likely to do so—for the kids themselves, for their parents, and for the rest of the world, insofar as it benefits from the kids' achievements.

In the case of Rufus and Dr. Jones, then, utilitarianism clashes with our common-sense views about morality, for our common-sense views include such ideas as that people have a right not to be deprived of their lives unless they have wronged society grievously. (Some would say that even then a person still has a right not to be deprived of his life, but we'll leave that issue aside for now.) Does this show that, although utilitarianism goes further than egoism in explaining what makes right acts right, it still does not go far enough? Perhaps not. Some might argue, at this point, that the present objection to the utilitarian theory stems from the fact that we are working with a simple-minded understanding of it. For perhaps the intermediate generalizations we mentioned in the last section should be taken as more than intermediate. After all, we did suggest that generally our following those intermediate generalizations will produce overall utility. So why don't we try to reformulate utilitarianism in terms that make crucial reference to those generalizations? Whereas utilitarianism, as we have formulated it so far, said this:

> *Act-Utilitarianism:* Perform that act, from those available, most likely to produce the greatest overall amount of happiness.

We may now consider another formulation:

[3] One version of the Hippocratic oath is as follows:

You do solemnly swear, each by whatever he or she holds most sacred,

That you will be loyal to the Profession of Medicine and just and generous to its members.

That you will lead your lives and practice your art in uprightness and honor.

That into whatsoever house you shall enter, it shall be for the good of the sick to the utmost of your power, your holding yourselves far aloof from wrong, from corruption, from the tempting of others to vice.

> *Rule-Utilitarianism:* Perform that act, from those available, that accords with a rule that is itself part of a system of rules the general following of which would produce the greatest overall amount of happiness.

While the system of rules envisioned by the rule-utilitarian is probably based on the sorts of precepts mentioned in the last section, it will be arrived at only after those rules have been checked out by our best sociologists, economists, psychologists, and others. Many years, and many billions of research dollars, may be required before we arrive at a satisfactory system of rules, but the task is presumably important enough that we should not shrink from undertaking it. This system of rules will be designed in such a way that it won't contain rules that give inconsistent directives. Further, it will be designed to be as complete as possible, so that few situations will arise in which the rules have no directives to offer. When new technologies are developed, or other innovations require the articulation of the rules to apply to the new cases, sociologists, economists, and others will have to reconvene to write more rules.

Rule-utilitarianism might seem an improvement on act-utilitarianism. After all, it gives a special place to moral principles having to do with rights and justice while it adheres to the importance of maximizing happiness. Further, it can explain why we feel Dr. Jones has done something wrong. After all, a general policy of euthanizing people for a short-term gain in utility will most likely result in an overall long-term loss; just consider the degree of insecurity such a policy would produce across society. However, it's not at all clear whether rule-utilitarianism, once its rules are clarified and refined, will be distinguishable from act-utilitarianism. Let us imagine our elite group of specialists convening for the first World Congress of Rule-Utilitarianism, charged with the task of developing a system of rules which, if generally followed, will maximize happiness. On the morning of the first day of the congress everyone fills up on muffins and coffee and takes

---

That you will exercise your art solely for the cure of your patients, and will give no drug, perform no operation, for a criminal purpose, even if solicited, far less suggest it.

That whatsoever you shall see or hear of the lives of men or women which is not fitting to be spoken, you will keep inviolably secret.

These things do you swear. Let each bow the head in sign of acquiescence.

And now, if you will be true to this, your oath, may prosperity and good repute be ever yours; the opposite, if you shall prove yourselves forsworn.

their seats by 9 AM sharp. After some opening remarks the first speaker, Delegate 1, offers the following suggestion for a first rule:

> Rule 1: Keep your promises.

Everyone applauds, and Rule 1 is projected onto a large screen. After a few minutes, however, Delegate 2 stands up and says:

> Ladies and gentlemen, Rule 1 is an excellent rule. However, it is too crude as it stands, for there will eventually come a case in which keeping one's promise will result in, say, the loss of one million lives. Our primary mission is the maximization of happiness, and following Rule 1 without qualification will eventually lead us away from that mission. Rather, I propose the following refinement of my esteemed colleague's rule:
>
> Rule 2: Keep your promises unless doing so will result in the loss of one or more million lives.

As before, everyone applauds, and now Rule 2 is projected onto the screen, superseding Rule 1. But after a few minutes Delegate 3 stands up and says:

> Ladies and gentlemen, Rule 2 is an excellent rule. However, it is too crude as it stands, for there will eventually come a case in which keeping one's promise will result in, say, the loss of half a million lives. Our primary mission is the maximization of happiness, and following Rule 2 without qualification will eventually lead us away from that mission. Rather, I propose the following refinement of my esteemed colleague's rule:
>
> Rule 3: Keep your promises unless doing so will result in the loss of half a million or more lives.

I think that by now you can imagine the rest of day one of the congress as well as a late-afternoon contribution like the following:

> Ladies and gentlemen, Rule 3268 is an excellent rule. However, it is too crude as it stands, for there will eventually come a case in which keeping one's promise will result in the production of less happiness than not keeping one's promise will have done. Our primary mission is the maximization of happiness, and following Rule 3268 without

> qualification will eventually lead us away from that mission. Rather, I propose the following refinement of my esteemed colleague's rule:
>
> Rule 3269: Keep your promises unless doing so will produce less happiness than not doing so would have done.

Now all the delegates look at each other dumbfounded, for they can see that Rule 3269 is equivalent to a rule that says:

> When deciding whether to keep one's promise, perform that act, from those available, most likely to produce the greatest overall amount of happiness.

The same line of reasoning would apply no matter which precept we started from, be it "Tell the truth," or "Do unto others as you would have done unto you," or whatever else. This shows that, no matter which precept they start with, after refining and improving that precept the delegates will always end up with a precept that gives no special weight to the fact that the act in question is an act of promise keeping, an act of truth telling, or anything else. Rather, in each case one will be told simply to do what the act-utilitarian does, namely, to perform that act, from those available, most likely to produce the greatest overall amount of happiness.

Our attempt to elucidate utilitarianism in terms not of acts but of rules, then, seems to be a dead end. If we try carefully to formulate a rule-utilitarian theory while respecting the importance of maximizing happiness, we can't help but revise it until it takes the form of an act-utilitarian theory. Accordingly, act-utilitarianism appears to be the only form of utilitarianism that is a contender for a viable ethical theory, and we are back once again to our problem of Rufus and Dr. Jones.

As we observed in our discussion of ethical egoism, our common-sense views are fallible. Maybe our common-sense belief that Dr. Jones has done something wrong in euthanizing Rufus is mistaken, like the once-common-sense view that the Earth is the center of the universe. But remember what Copernicus did: He was able to show that the heliocentric theory of the universe better accounts for the empirical data than does the geocentric theory, justifying giving up the common-sense geocentric theory. What evidence might the utilitarian adduce to show that our ordinary intuitions about morality are wrong? It's hard to see what empirical evidence we could bring forth to show that, for instance, contrary to your initial reaction, Dr. Jones really did the right thing. Until we find such evidence, we do well to continue searching for a better answer to the question, what makes right acts right?

Intermission: Moral Relativism

Many readers will feel that our entire discussion of ethics got off on the wrong foot in seeking for a single, overarching answer to the question, what makes right acts right? After all, it might be said, just affixing a question mark to a sentence doesn't guarantee that we are asking a meaningful question. In fact, a person might think she is asking a meaningful question but she might be wrong. Imagine someone devotes her life to answering the question, what is the largest integer? She's confused. There is no largest integer. For any integer N that you find, you can find an even bigger one in N+1. Or you might for a moment think that the following is a meaningful question: what time is it at the center of the Milky Way? After all, it makes sense to ask what time it is in Detroit, in Kuala Lumpur, and in Vladivostok. But of course, our system of timekeeping is only defined for various spots on Earth and makes no sense once we leave the planet, to say nothing of the solar system.

So there are questions that seem to make sense, but really do not. Many will now urge that the question, what makes right acts right? is another one of these. Just as the question, what time is it in place so-and-so? only makes sense relative to a system of timekeeping, perhaps questions of right and wrong only make sense relative to one or another frame of reference such as a society, a culture, an ethnicity, or even an individual. I propose now to take a brief intermission from our survey of ethical theories to consider this idea that morality is in some sense or other "relative." As we'll see, this relativist position may be seen not as an answer to the question, what makes right acts right? but rather as a constraint on any successful answer to that question.

As justification for this relativist position, we might remember the vast difference of opinion across space and time about what is right and what is wrong. For some societies, it is perfectly acceptable to eat other human beings; for others it is taboo. For some societies, children are considered to be of inestimable value; in other societies, including many in the past, they are not even considered persons until they are at least five years old. In some cultures women have many husbands, yet in others a man might have many wives.

Observations like these are the stock in trade of cultural anthropology. One cannot read more than a few pages in this field without being amazed at the variety of moral systems by which cultures have abided over time and even by which cultures abide across the world at this time. Notice that cultural anthropology, when it offers data of this sort, offers empirical data about the range of opinions on certain matters of right and wrong. Let us give this form of relativism a name:

> *Quotidian moral relativism:* There are a considerable variety of opinions on questions of right and wrong throughout space and time.

Quotidian moral relativism is incredibly well confirmed by the data gathered by cultural anthropologists. Perhaps there are some underlying uniformities of opinion on ethical matters across cultures, both temporally and spatially, but even if that's true we still find a great deal of variation, and this is all that quotidian moral relativism claims. However, when relativism is discussed in ethics, a stronger position is usually in the back of people's minds. According to this stronger position, it is not just that opinions vary dramatically as to what is right and what is wrong but that no one of these opinions is more right than any of the others. Rather, asking the question, Is cannibalism *really* wrong? is like asking, Is it *really* midnight? This latter question doesn't make sense unless you specify your time zone on Earth, and, of course, it makes no sense at all once you leave this planet. So too, one might say, the question whether cannibalism is really wrong doesn't make sense unless you specify a culture, ethnicity, society, or other point of view. Then, just as it might be definitely either true or false to claim that it is midnight in Boston on eastern standard time, so too it can now be definitely either true or false to claim that cannibalism is right relative to Aztec society, the Binderwurs of Central India, the Fore of Papua New Guinea, or suburban Minneapolis. The form of relativism we are now considering seems more robust than quotidian relativism, and I'll anoint it with an appropriate title:

> *Robust moral relativism:* There is no perspective-independent fact of the matter as to what is right or wrong; rather, the only facts about morality that hold are relative to a point of view. (This point of view might

be constituted by a society, a culture, an ethnicity, or even an individual, and different forms of robust relativism will flow from different ways of understanding what sorts of entities moral facts are relative to.)

It is crucial that we are clear about the relation between quotidian and robust relativism. First of all, quotidian relativism does not imply robust relativism. We can accept that there is a great deal of variation across space and through time in opinions about what is right and what is wrong without being committed to robust relativism. To see why, consider this analogy: Opinions about the causes of disease vary considerably across space and through time. Some think that disease is due to evil spirits; others think it is due to the wrath of the gods; others think it is due to the work of Satan; others think it is due to such things as bacteria and viruses. I'm sure there are other opinions as well about what makes people, plants, and animals sick. However, all these differing opinions do not for a moment show that there is no perspective-independent fact of the matter with regard to what causes disease. For instance, if you thought that a baby is sick because she has a streptococcus infection, you probably wouldn't take very seriously the suggestion that your opinion is a matter of your perspective or point of view. Rather, you'd probably feel that there is something or other that has made the baby sick, and we need to know what that something is if we are to save her life. Choosing one perspective or another is not going to make any difference to what is really causing her to be ill.

Quotidian relativism about a subject matter doesn't imply robust relativism about that subject matter. What, then, would justify inferring from quotidian relativism in ethics—a view that is eminently plausible—to robust relativism in ethics, given that that inference is not itself logically compulsory? The only way one might hope to get from the quotidian premise to the robust conclusion is to add more premises, or at least ideas that could be turned into relevant premises, so I will suggest some.

"Who's to say?"

Once we recognize the variety of opinions about morality that are articulated in quotidian moral relativism, we should see that we can't hope to justify one of these opinions as superior to the others. I personally am no fan of cannibalism, and in fact I think it is wrong. However, if some other society, such as the Fore of Papua New

Guinea, has cannibalism deeply embedded into its cultural practices, one might ask, "Who are you to say that the Fore are wrong? Wouldn't doing so reinstate the very cultural imperialism that Western society is now trying to move beyond?"

We might reply: We each have our convictions. Not all of those convictions can be proven beyond a shadow of a doubt, either conceptually or on the basis of empirical or mathematical evidence. However, as we observed in Chapter 1, a central feature of philosophy is its search for justifications of controversial opinions that might not be settled one way or another a priori or by empirical investigation. Such justifications can be reasonable without constituting conclusive proof. In a matter such as cannibalism, we can justify its prohibition on such grounds as that people have a right not to be deprived of their lives in order to become someone's dinner or the centerpiece of a ritual.

A reply to the "who's to say?" basis for robust relativism is, then, that without setting myself as a higher authority on morality than anyone else in the world, I can still give reasons for my moral convictions, and those reasons may be the basis of my view that some other ways of living are immoral. I would expect it to be equally possible for someone in a different society to have a justified moral criticism of my own lifestyle: the amount of energy I consume, the sort of food I eat, the way I raise my children might all be the target of justifiable criticism. I would like to think that if I heard that criticism and found it persuasive, I would change aspects of my life and be grateful to have been enlightened. So, too, I can criticize the practices of others without pretending that I have some special access to the truth about morality. Rather, we all have our convictions, and we are all equally entitled to use our reasoning to support those convictions as best we can.

The "who's to say?" question does not seem an adequate basis for jumping to robust relativism. What else might be?

"We shouldn't sit in judgment of others"

It might be held that if we are not robust relativists, we will be prone to sit in judgment of others. The unspoken assumption here, of course, is that doing so would be wrong. We may make two observations about this idea. First of all, the robust relativist must be taking at least one moral doctrine as true no matter what one's perspective, namely, that it is wrong to sit in judgment of others. If she did not do that, she would at most be able to say that this proscription is correct relative to some points of view, incorrect relative to others. But then, I might adopt a point of view that does not accept this proscription. In that case this proscription will not move me at all.

Second, the moral imperative that we should not sit in judgment of others is naturally understood to mean that to do so is to put yourself up as having Godlike access to the truths of morality. What a lot of nerve! Isn't it pompous to go around telling people how they should live?

Let's take these ideas carefully, though. I can believe that someone is doing something wrong without thinking for a moment that I am superior to them or thinking that I have a Godlike access to the truths of morality. Down the street is a neighbor who regularly uses corporal punishment on his children. This punishment does not break bones, nor does it in other ways merit the attention of the Department of Social Services. I nevertheless think it is wrong to punish children physically, and I have some reasons that justify that view. What is important, however, is that I can think it is wrong to punish children physically without for a moment believing that I am superior to people who do use corporal punishment. So, too, you might think that in being a carnivore I am behaving in an immoral way, and you will probably have your reasons for being a vegetarian. Here too, though, you can think that I am immoral in eating meat without thinking that you are morally superior to me. I conclude that we can refrain from robust relativism without sitting in judgment of others. Below is a final attempt to justify robust moral relativism.

"Robust relativism is the only way of respecting the integrity and autonomy of other cultures, ethnicities, and societies"

It might be held that only the robust moral relativist can truly respect the integrity and autonomy of other cultures, societies, etc. Holding that things are only right or wrong relative to a point of view, would seem to suggest that I will be more likely to respect ways of life that differ from my own.

I want directly to challenge the idea that only the robust relativist can respect ways of life that differ from her own. Let us return to the neighbor down the street who uses corporal punishment on his children. I can think that what he does is morally wrong without for a moment feeling tempted to call in the police, the social workers, or anyone else. Even though some ways of treating children might in my opinion be improper, I respect other values, such as the ability of a family to make its own choices without the interference of the state. Likewise, to take a case on a much larger scale, in many countries women's status is inferior to men's, and that status hierarchy is supported by the government. My own conviction is that women should be accorded the same status as men in every society, but this does not mean that I am committed to advocating attacking or boycotting a country that does not share this view in order to make it change its ways. The reason is that respect for a nation's autonomy is one among many values that I cherish, along with respect for women. As a result, trying to intervene in another person's, family's, or country's affairs in order to get them to behave as I think they ought is often unjustified; at the very least that impulse needs to be set alongside the importance of autonomy and self-determination.

We have tried three different ways of supporting the inference from quotidian moral relativism to robust moral relativism, all without apparent success. However, our efforts have not been wasted, and this for two reasons: First, we can now see that one can be an objectivist about morality—that is, hold that what is right or wrong is not relative to one's point of view—without believing that one's own moral convictions are any more important than anyone else's, without sitting in judgment of others, and without violating the integrity and autonomy of other cultures, ethnicities, and societies. That doesn't mean that moral objectivism is true, and we have certainly not shown that robust moral relativism is untrue. What we have seen, however, is that the unquestionable truth of quotidian moral relativism does not, even with further plausible principles, mandate acceptance of robust moral relativism.

Second, even if robust moral relativism is true, that does not exempt any person, culture, or other point of view from the need to examine its own convictions to see if they hold up under scrutiny. For instance, the society that Aldous Huxley imagines in *Brave New World* is utilitarian. If robust moral relativism is true, then the right thing to do in that society is to act on utilitarian principles. Nonetheless, at any given time a character in the society portrayed in Huxley's novel might come along to ask whether utilitarian moral principles are correct. She or he might find reason to challenge the reigning morality and propose an alternative. Granted, such a dissenter in *Brave New World* is likely to be liquidated pretty quickly, but that may not be the case in actual, nonfictional societies with a dominant moral system.

Because of this, even a robust moral relativist has good reason to pay attention to a discussion of various moral theories such as the one finds in the non-intermission parts of this chapter. One never knows when it might make sense to reset one's watches. End of intermission.

Kantian Ethics

Thus far we've considered two answers to the question, what makes right acts right? The first answer was ethical egoism; the second was utilitarianism. A final answer to this question takes its inspiration from the idea that eating someone as a ritual, euthanizing a vagrant, and so on are wrong not because of some bad consequences that might flow from such actions, but rather because they fail to pay adequate respect to people. For instance, when Dr. Jones takes Rufus' life in order to save the lives of talented children, he is putting the value of those children's lives over that of Rufus. Granted, we don't expect the world to benefit greatly from Rufus, but that doesn't seem like a good enough reason to use him as a dispensable means to some other admittedly valuable end result. Dr. Jones has not treated Rufus respectfully. So, too, using another person as a meal seems like treating him as a stepping-stone to some other end, namely, my nutrition. That doesn't seem to treat him respectfully either.

Behind the idea that we should treat others with respect is a form of the Golden Rule. I am sure that you can remember times as a child when someone asked, "How would you like it if someone did that to you?" To reply, "I wouldn't. But no one is doing that to me, so what do I care?" would not be much of an answer. Rather, the person who raised the question is implicitly suggesting that the perpetrator should have treated others in the way that he himself would want to be treated. A person's respect for himself or herself will suggest that she would want others to treat her with respect, and if she wants to behave properly, she will treat others with respect as well.

A central idea behind so-called deontological ethics is this idea of impartiality: I don't merit any special treatment as either above or below others. Rather, I should act toward others in the way that I would want them to act toward me. One consequence of this is a principle deriving from the philosopher Immanuel Kant (1724–1804):

> *Formula of the End in Itself*
> Act in such a way that you always treat humanity, whether in your own person or in the person of any other, never simply as a means but always at the same time as an end.[4]

This norm has no problem with treating someone as a means. I ask you to hold something for me for a moment, and in so doing I am using you as a means to an end that I am trying to achieve. But I am not treating you as a *mere* means, for there is nothing in this request that fails to treat you respectfully, particularly if I say "please." On the other hand, if someone is shooting at me and I grab you to use you as a shield to protect myself, then I am treating you not only as a means but also as a mere means. For here I am not treating you with respect. Instead I am acting as if my own life is more important than yours, even though we are both human beings, and that doesn't seem respectful of you.

Take another example: I promise to pay you a certain sum of money in return for your car, and before I pay you the money you give me your car. Here I am using you as a means to my end (owning a car), but nothing is wrong with this because no particular disrespect comes from my using you to acquire a car. On the other hand, if I make a lying promise in the same transaction, with no intention of paying up after receiving the car, then our ordinary instincts say that I have exploited or abused the trust that you placed in me. I surely wouldn't like to be so used. This, however, in turn shows that in making that lying promise I have used you not only as a means but also as a mere means, for I am acting as if my own interests are more important than yours. Structurally, the situation is like the one in which I use your body to shield myself from bullets.

Kant even thinks that it is possible to violate the Formula of the End in Itself in the way you treat yourself. He gives the example of a person who is feeling so discouraged about his life that he contemplates suicide. According to Kant, in committing suicide this person will be treating himself not only as a means, but also as a mere means, because while suicide may achieve his aim of relieving suffering, he will also be failing to respect himself. He fails to respect the fact that he has talents that might be developed and used for good once he gets over his slump. Instead, all he cares about is getting over his current

[4] Immanuel Kant, *Groundwork for the Metaphysics of Morals,* translated by H. Paton. New York: Harper and Row, 1964, p. 95.

bout of suffering in the easiest way, and that's by slitting his wrists. Here, unlike the cases of the human shield and the lying promise, the suicide is not treating himself as more important than himself. That, after all, doesn't seem to be possible. Rather, the suicide is treating his own *desire for suffering-reduction* as more important than his potential for *developing talents and helping others*. In this way he is being disrespectful of his own self. I suspect that Kant would offer a similar criticism of someone who never tries hard to better himself but instead spends his life in an unchallenging job simply because that is the path of least resistance.

Utilitarianism and deontological ethics share the following feature: Both place value on the well-being of others rather than on one's own well-being. For the utilitarian, her own happiness is no more important than anyone else's as a consideration for what she should do. For the deontologist, his own interests are no more important than anyone else's, and if the deontologist treats his own interests as if they are more important than another's, he is liable to treat others as mere means. However, utilitarian ethics and deontological ethics part company quite dramatically in other ways. For instance, while the utilitarian seems to have to allow cases in which she should sacrifice her rights in service to the many, the deontologist will stand firm against this way of acting. He will say, for instance, that Dr. Jones has used Rufus as a mere means, and that is why Dr. Jones has acted wrongly. Similarly, the deontologist will say that if people have what we would normally feel are wicked pleasures, such as pleasure over watching others suffering, those pleasures have no moral value, because they treat people as mere means. By contrast, the utilitarian has no small challenge explaining why some forms of happiness are more "valid" than others.

Here is another contrast between these two ethical theories: The utilitarian focuses on the consequences of actions, and in fact Mill tells us that motives are not relevant to whether an act is right or wrong. By contrast, the deontologist is not primarily concerned about consequences; rather, he is concerned about how we treat other people, and at the center of this idea of how you treat someone is the principle on which you act. If I act on the principle, "Use someone else's body to shield myself from harm," I am behaving immorally. Kant thinks that the same is true if I act on the principle, "Make a lying promise if you think you can get away with it." He actually promotes the importance of principles into the following overarching idea:

Categorical Imperative
Act only on those principles that you would will to see followed by all humanity.

This is Kant's reformulation of the Golden Rule for his ethical theory. It builds in the kind of impartiality that we mentioned earlier. For instance, I certainly wouldn't want everyone to act on the principle, "Make a lying promise if you think you can get away with it," for eventually I will end up on the business end of that principle. Nor would I want to be in danger of being used as a human shield. Instead, the categorical imperative requires that I treat myself as one bit of humanity, neither greater nor less than others, and act accordingly.

We might clarify the Categorical Imperative by distinguishing it from the idea that we sometimes hear in criticism of an action, "What if everyone did that?" It is really awful to throw trash out of a car window whenever it's convenient, for if everyone did that, we'd have a much more polluted world than we already have. However, it is not so clear why the "What if everyone did that?" question is relevant to proving that doing this is wrong. For if someone asked me the "What if everyone did that?" question after I littered in this way, I'd reply as follows: "It would be really bad if everyone did that. But I have no reason to think that everyone will do that, so what's the problem?" It is difficult to see how the person who has criticized my littering would respond to this.

On the other hand, the Categorical Imperative goes a bit deeper. It doesn't suggest for a moment that when I act on a certain principle I have reason to think that everyone else will follow suit. Rather, it suggests that when I act in a certain way I might, or then again might not, be treating myself as more important than others. If I am treating myself as more important than others, then I am violating the Categorical Imperative and should reconsider the principle behind my action.

We have seen problems with ethical egoism and utilitarianism, and we have had trouble finding a good reason for accepting robust moral relativism even if quotidian moral relativism seems correct. Is deontological ethics the key to morality? We do not yet know enough to say for sure. One difficulty that vexes deontological theory is the very way in which it puts principles over consequences. Suppose it is now noon, and you, the mayor, have just found out that a terrorist has set bombs all over the city of Chicago, all set to go off this evening at 6:00 PM. The terrorist is nowhere to be found, there's no prospect of defusing the bombs in time, and if we tell the city's populace to leave, the resulting mayhem will cause huge loss of life. On the other hand, if the bombs go off as many as a million lives will be lost.

Your advisors present you with one possible solution. They know how to get their hands on the terrorist's daughter, Susie, and they know, based on a psychological profile of the terrorist, that she is his only truly weak spot. (This terrorist has been in and out of institutions for the criminally insane for years, and we know his emotional makeup rather well.) If we can find his daughter and start torturing her, there is a very good chance that the terrorist will capitulate and help us defuse the bombs. We can't fake it: The terrorist had an earlier career in computer graphics, and he will know if we try some virtual reality or animation stunt. We really have to torture Susie to within an inch of her life if he is to break. It seems, then, that we are faced with the choice of allowing the bombs to go off, resulting in the loss of possibly a million lives, and torturing the terrorist's daughter to within an inch of her life even though she is perfectly innocent.

A utilitarian will waste no time in deciding what to do here: He will say you should torture the little girl. After all, her suffering is pretty minor compared with the amount of happiness that will be lost if the bombs go off. The situation is structurally similar to that of Rufus and Dr. Jones, except on a larger and more dramatic scale. On the other hand, a deontological position will seem to tell us to keep our hands off Susie. After all, torturing her would be treating her as a mere means, namely to saving the lives of the inhabitants of Chicago. Further, any principle on which we act, if we choose to torture her, would seem to be one that we couldn't wish to see followed universally. (How could it apply to her without at the same time, for instance, telling us to kill Rufus for his organs?) But, on the other hand, if we follow the deontological principle in this case, we will refrain from torturing the little girl and we will perhaps lose a million lives. Is that acceptable? If it is, what if the case were changed so that you'd have to torture the girl to prevent thermonuclear bombs from detonating all over the world? Would it *then* be okay to torture Susie?

Your advisors may even entreat you in this way: "Mrs. (Mr.) Mayor, the lives of around one million Chicagoans will be on your head if you sit and do nothing to the terrorist's daughter. But we can get her in our custody in just moments, and we beg you to give us the order to start working on her!" You feel the sweat dripping down your forehead and notice that you've got no more fingernails left to bite. What will you do?

Study Questions

1. Consider the question, what makes right acts right? How would an ethical egoist answer this question? How would a utilitarian answer this question? (In your discussion, it will be helpful to explain how both theories make use of the idea of maximizing expected utility.)

2. Explain the objection to Bentham's version of utilitarianism, that it is a theory "worthy of swine." Next, explain why Mill holds that a proper form of utilitarianism needs to take into account the fact that some pleasures are higher than others. What is Mill's test for determining which pleasures are higher than others?

3. One objection to Mill's form of utilitarianism is that it sets too high a standard for humanity. Please explain Mill's response to this objection.

4. One objection to Mill's theory is that we rarely have time to calculate and weigh the effects of a prospective action on the general happiness. How does Mill reply to this objection?

5. In Chapter Two of *Utilitarianism,* Mill emphasizes the value of making statements when he refers to "the trustworthiness of human assertion, which is not only the principal support of all present social well-being, but the insufficiency of which does more than any one thing that can be named to keep back civilization, virtue, everything on which human happiness on the largest scale depends." That is pretty high praise. Does Mill hold that utilitarianism nevertheless sometimes requires one to tell a lie? Please explain your answer.

6. Could a utilitarian use her ethical theory to justify placing limitations on the use of (nonhuman) animals for the development of cosmetics to be used by human beings? Please explain your answer. Next, please distinguish between the following two major forms of justification for the punishment of criminals: retribution and deterrence. (By "criminal" let us mean a person who is known to have

broken a law that is itself a morally acceptable law.) Would a utilitarian tend to favor one form of justification over another? Please explain your answer.

7. E. F. Carritt, in an article entitled, "Criticisms of Utilitarianism,"[5] sums up his dissatisfaction with utilitarianism as follows: "In short, utilitarianism has forgotten rights; it allows no right to a man because he is innocent or because he has worked hard or has been promised or injured, or because he stands in any other special relation to us." (We may assume that his point applies to women as well!) Explain why Carritt might make this criticism, and Carritt's reasons for making it. In your answer, please give an example of how utilitarianism would seem to require forgetting someone's rights.

8. John Stuart Mill may be read as espousing a version of rule-utilitarianism rather than act-utilitarianism. Explain the difference between these two theories. Explain why one might be tempted to espouse rule-utilitarianism in light of some of the difficulties with act-utilitarianism. Next, why might it be said that rule-utilitarianism is "unstable," reducing ultimately to act-utilitarianism?

9. Please distinguish between "quotidian" and "robust" forms of moral relativism. Does quotidian moral relativism imply that there is no objective matter of fact about what is right and what is wrong? Please explain your answer. Next, suppose you find some people's behavior immoral, such as the cannibalism of the Fore of Papua New Guinea, even though that behavior does not harm you. Is being a robust moral relativist the *only* way in which you could consistently justify refraining from intervening in their lives? That is, is robust moral relativism the only way in which you could consistently justify a "live and let live" policy? Please explain your answer.

10. Kant espouses the Formula of the End in Itself, which states,

> Act in such a way that you always treat humanity, whether in your own person or in the person of any other, never simply as a means but always at the same time as an end.

What is the difference between treating a person as a means and treating that person as a mere means? Please illustrate your answer with examples. In your answer to these questions, please explain the

[5] E. F. Carritt, "Criticisms of Utilitarianism." *Ethical and Political Thinking*. Oxford: Oxford University Press, 1947.

relevance of whether the person in question can consent to being treated in a certain way. Could the Formula of the End in Itself explain why we think that some kinds of suicide are morally wrong? Please explain your answer.

Suggestions for Further Reading

The early chapters of Plato's *Republic* contain a dramatic discussion between Socrates and Thrasymachus, who defends a form of ethical egoism. Plato, *Republic,* translated by C.D.C. Reeve. Indianapolis: Hackett Publishing Company, 2004.

Jeremy Bentham's best-known formulation of utilitarianism can be found in *The Classical Utilitarians: Bentham and Mill,* edited by John Troyer. Indianapolis: Hackett Publishing Company, 2003.

John Stuart Mill's *Utilitarianism,* 2nd edition, edited by G. Sher (Indianapolis: Hackett Publishing Company, 2002) is a classic, because of both its historical importance and its accessibility to the modern reader.

J.J.C. Smart and B. Williams, *Utilitarianism: For and Against.* Cambridge: Cambridge University Press, 1973.

P. Singer, ed. *A Companion to Ethics*. Oxford: Blackwell Publishers, 1991.

Immanuel Kant's classic introduction to his ethical theory is in his *Grounding of the Metaphysics of Morals,* 3rd edition, edited by J. Ellington. Indianapolis: Hackett Publishing Company, 1993.

A good collection of essays on moral relativism is P. Moser and T. Carson, *Moral Relativism: A Reader*. New York: Oxford University Press, 2001.

Aldous Huxley's *Brave New World* (Cutchogue, NY: Buccaneer Books, 1991) is a society based on utilitarian principles.

Movies Significant for Ethics

There are a vast number of movies that confront ethical issues. Some that stand out include

Crimes and Misdemeanors (1989), directed by Woody Allen.

Do the Right Thing (1989), directed by Spike Lee.

5. The Matter of Minds

In Chapter 3, we mentioned the theory of evolution by natural selection as a challenge to the argument from design, a famous attempt to justify belief in the Greatest Conceivable Being. Evolution by natural selection seems to do a respectable job of accounting for a great deal of biological complexity, but it has not fully succeeded in accounting for the complexity of the mind, or at least certain aspects of it. More precisely, at the time of this writing it cannot be confidently claimed that we have a full biological account of phenomena such as consciousness. This is not to say that such an account is impossible. Perhaps it is. However, one of the most hotly contested areas of contemporary philosophy, as well as related areas of psychology and neuroscience, attempts to give a biological explanation of all features of human and animal minds. It is also the province of the philosophy of mind, the focus of this chapter.

We will consider a few historically important ways of thinking about the mind before we approach the contemporary scene. Then we will explain the challenge minds seem to pose for an attempt to understand the world in purely materialistic terms. Along the way we will discuss some historically significant views of the mind's relation to matter, as well as some ways that experimental psychology bears on our knowledge of ourselves.

Plato's Tripartite Soul

We encountered Plato in Chapter 3, where we discussed whether it makes sense to think that God created morality; Plato recorded a discussion that Socrates is reputed to have had with Euthyphro, who was prosecuting his father for murdering a slave. Later in his life Plato began to work out his own views rather than report the views of Socrates, but to promote those ideas he hit upon the clever device of writing dialogues that appeared to be records of conversations that Socrates had with his friends. In these dialogues Plato would have the fictional character Socrates propound views that were actually Plato's own. (My expert colleagues assure me that Plato's contemporaries would have been in on the trick.)

One such dialogue is the *Republic.* Socrates and his friends are discussing what it is to be just, and to answer this question Socrates launches into a lengthy investigation of what we would now call the mind—what Plato has Socrates call the soul. Socrates proposes that the soul is organized in a way analogous to the parts of an ideal city-state he imagines, the *kallipolis.* In the kallipolis, Socrates tells us, we find three classes of citizens: the rulers, the guardians or soldiers, and the producers—farmers, artisans, and the like. According to Socrates, the job of rulers is the attainment of wisdom and the proper organization of the kallipolis. The job of the guardians is the defense of the honor and safety of the kallipolis. The job of the producers is the fulfillment of the citizens' appetites for food and other goods and services.

Socrates also suggests a corresponding tripartition of the individual soul into a rational part, a spirited part, and an appetitive part. The latter seeks gratification of the senses with food, sex, and the like. The spirited part is the home of emotion: It gets angry when we are insulted and prepares us to fight to defend our honor if need be. The rational part seeks wisdom as well as the proper coordination of the other two parts of the soul for the smooth running of the person.

Plato seems not to have been concerned with determining what a mind is and how it relates to the rest of nature. Rather, he was interested in understanding which forms of mental organization produce the most fulfilling life. He suggests, for example, that one whose appetitive part dominates the other two parts ends up being a slave of the flesh, a glutton. One whose spirited part dominates is like Jake LaMotta of the movie *Raging Bull:* a hothead, always ready to fight at the slightest provocation. Plato does not advocate that the rational part squelch the other two. That would be a form of asceticism foreign to Plato and his culture. Instead, Plato holds that the rational part of the soul should be in control of the other two parts, but should also give those other two parts their due: If I am insulted, I should defend my honor, and I should satisfy my bodily needs so long as I do so with moderation. Dysfunction occurs only when spirit or appetite murders reason to take the throne of the self.

Our interest in this chapter is not in how to live a happy life, so we will pursue no further the question how best to organize the parts of the soul. Instead, I've brought up Plato to suggest that his tripartition of the soul is prescient. More exactly, with some refinements and modifications his distinctions survive today in a fairly widely accepted way of carving up mental phenomena into the *cognitive,* the *affective,* and the *experiential.* The cognitive part of our minds, corresponding to Plato's rational part, has to do with belief, knowledge, and information, including both information we are now receiving and information we retain through memory. The affective part of our minds, corresponding to Plato's appetitive part, has to do with moods and emotions. The experiential aspect of our minds, loosely corresponding to Plato's appetitive part, has to do with the way things look, taste, smell, etc. To set this out a bit more vividly, imagine you're gazing at an orange on a table before you. You know that an orange is in front of you, as well as, roughly how big it is and how far away it is. These achievements are the province of the cognitive component of the mind. The orange might also remind you of the color of the shoes a certain person wore on your first date; with luck it will also bring up fond memories and thus activate the affective part of the mind. Finally, as you contemplate the orange you attend to its color, perhaps reach out to feel its texture, and then peel it to eat a slice. Experiences of the color, the texture and the taste of the orange are all examples of the experiential parts of the mind. Understanding the cognitive, affective, and experiential components of the mind are among the most important undertakings of contemporary philosophy of mind, psychology, and neuroscience.

Descartes' Division

It may come as a surprise that only in the last few decades have the affective and experiential components of the mind become a topic of serious philosophical research. One reason may be that the last few centuries of philosophy were dominated by a tradition flowing from René Descartes (1596–1650), whose most famous works focus on the cognitive component of the mind. (To his credit, Descartes did write a book on the affective part entitled *The Passions of the Soul,* but this work was less influential than his other writings.) While Plato was concerned with how best to live a happy life, Descartes was concerned with how best to secure a foundation for our knowledge of the world. His focus on knowledge naturally emphasizes the cognitive component of the mind over the affective and the experiential.

Descartes begins his *Meditations on First Philosophy* with the observation that he's not so sure now of a lot of things he took as obvious in his youth. Imagine for instance that you were raised on the Ptolemaic system of astronomy, according to which the Earth is the center of the universe. Then you get to college, only to learn that nothing of the kind is true: The Sun is the center of our solar system, which is a puny bit of a much vaster galaxy that is, in turn, one among unimaginably many galaxies. That realization would come as a shock, not least because it might make you wonder which of your other cherished beliefs you need to overthrow as well. Descartes imagines someone trying to minimize the shock of this realization by responding: "Well look, you can't doubt that you're here reading these words or that 2+2=4! What could be more obvious than these things?" Descartes' reply is both ingenious and disturbing: How can you rule out the possibility that your thoughts are being controlled by some external force that makes you *think* that you're awake reading words, and that makes you *think* that 2 added to 2 gives 4? Anything you might try to use as proof that these things are not happening itself already assumes that you're not being deceived and so generates our question all over again. For example, you might say, "Well, I can pinch myself and feel the pain, and that will show that I'm awake." The trouble is that this experience of feeling the pinch could itself be part of a very vivid dream or, instead, could have been planted in your mind by that external force we mentioned above.

Please take a moment to let these questions sink in. At first it will seem crazy to admit that you can't be quite sure that you're awake reading words. But if you've ever had a very vivid dream you might have been convinced at the time that what it represented was in fact true. (You can be pretty sure this is happening with people you observe yelling, crying, or screaming in their sleep.) Again, if you've seen the movie *The Matrix,* you'll have a vivid sense of how someone might have experiences that have been synthesized with such accuracy that she is sure she is living a normal life as a worker in a big city when in fact she is in a pod generating energy for machines! So how do you know that's not happening to you right now?

I confess I don't know how to answer this question. I really have no idea what incontrovertible evidence I can point to that would rule out this depressing possibility. I do feel *sure* that I'm not in a pod generating energy for machines, but I don't know how to show that I'm not. Descartes thought he could. He asks us first of all to consider the difference between my seeing an orange and my seeming to see an orange. I may not be able to be sure that I am in fact seeing an orange; maybe I'm being duped by some malevolent machine into thinking that I am. However, even if I'm being duped, even if my mind is being manipulated by some external force, I can be dead sure that it *seems* to me as if there is an orange before me. Contemporary philosophers call this process of knowing the contents of our own minds *introspection*. According to Descartes, even if I am being duped about what is going on outside my mind, introspection never errs: If something is in my mind, such as a pain, an emotion, a thought, or even an apparent sensation of something outside of me, then I must be aware of it. Further, if introspection tells me that something is in my mind, then it is. Whether I can be certain of anything outside of my mind is a question he takes on later.

Not only can I be sure about the contents of my mind, Descartes argues, I can also be sure that I exist. The reason is that, once again, even if I am being deceived mercilessly, I can't be being deceived without existing. If I'm being deceived, I'm still thinking, and I can't do that without being there to do the thinking. This line of thought has been enshrined in popular culture to the point of making its way onto T-shirts in the slogan,

> Cogito, ergo sum.

This is Latin for the argument:

> I am thinking, therefore I exist.

The argument is valid: It's not possible to think without existing too! In addition, at least while I am considering the question, the premise "I am thinking" seems true. Descartes puts the point nicely:

> Here I make my discovery: thought exists; it alone cannot be separated from me. I am; I exist—this is certain. But for how long? For as long as I am thinking; for perhaps it could also come to pass that if I were to cease all thinking I would then utterly cease to exist. (*Meditations on First Philosophy*, p. 19)

Here Descartes tells me that I can introspect on the fact that I am thinking. From this I may infer that I exist. (He also seems to hold that if I cease to think, I will cease to exist, but this is a further claim that we need not dwell upon here.) So we can be sure of at least two things, Descartes argues: the contents of our minds, and, on that basis, that we exist. That might seem a pretty paltry foundation on which to construct a theory of the mind or anything else, but Descartes has further ideas at his disposal. He next gives an elaborate argument for the existence of a GCB that I won't recapitulate here. Suffice it to say that this argument makes him certain that a GCB exists. He also gleans from this argument some conclusions about the possibility of evil. Assume with Descartes that error is a kind of evil. When I am wrong about something—the cause of epilepsy, the reason why my old friend hasn't called me, the future of the stock market—that is a failing. Perhaps it is not the worst possible failing, but it does seem a bad thing nonetheless, a shortcoming in the world. This seems to be what Descartes has in mind in thinking of error as an evil. In addition, normally when we are in error it is our own fault: We have miscalculated, drawn a hasty conclusion, or misremembered something. On the other hand, suppose that we have used our rational faculties to the very best of our abilities. We have checked our calculations again and again, guarded against bias and prejudice, and so on. Descartes holds that if we do all these things, then the GCB would be to blame if we *still* end up being in error. After all, such an error is an evil, and it can't be blamed on us. Descartes thinks that in such a case, the GCB would have to be responsible for the error. He formulates this in the famous

> *Doctrine of Clear and Distinct Perception:* Whatever I clearly and distinctly perceive is true.

"Clear and distinct perception" is code for the idea that I've done my utmost to ensure that my reasoning is accurate. If I have done that, then the doctrine of clear and distinct perception tells me that I *can't* go wrong. Standing on its own the doctrine might look like wishful thinking. However, keep in mind the theological background: If you can be absolutely sure—as Descartes was by the time he formulated his doctrine—that the GCB exists, then you might reasonably conclude that any evil that there is must be due to mankind; it can't be due to the GCB lest He be something short of the Greatest Conceivable. But if that is right, then if I can also be sure that I've done my utmost to be intellectually virtuous, then I can't possibly be wrong.[1]

[1] Recalling our discussion of the problem of evil in Chapter 3, you might notice that Descartes is assuming that a GCB would create the very best possible world that was within Its power to create. Recalling our example of the goldfish and the puppies, you might doubt that that assumption is correct.

Now we're ready to understand Descartes' legacy for our study of the mind. I'll bet you can conceive of disembodied existence. Maybe it's hard to imagine such a thing, just like it's hard to imagine curved space-time or the size of our galaxy. It nevertheless seems conceivable that a person could survive the destruction of her body. People who think that life after death is at least possible seem to admit this. Further, notice that you can admit this possibility without being a theist. Even an agnostic or atheist might agree that the idea of disembodied existence seems conceivable. Descartes would make this point by saying that we can clearly and distinctly conceive of the mind existing without the body. If that's right, though, then his doctrine of clear and distinct perception allows us to conclude that the one *can* exist without the other.

So what? Well, if x and y are identical, then they have all their characteristics in common. (This is known as the indiscernibility of identicals.) Hence, if you can find an x and a y that don't have all their characteristics in common, you can be sure that they are not identical, that is, that they are distinct. Now consider properties having to do with capacities. Take my word for it: My Newfoundland dog can eat an entire Thanksgiving turkey in less than ten minutes. She has that capacity even if she is not exercising that capacity at the moment. (She happens to be snoozing on the rug right now, but I'm sure she still has that capacity.) So too, Descartes would point out, my mind has the capacity of existing without my body; that was the gist of our conclusion a moment ago, that the mind can exist without the body. But of course my body doesn't have that capacity—my body can't exist without my body. But then my mind and my body have different properties, and so are not identical. Here is that argument put more formally:

1. If x=y, then x and y have all their properties in common.
2. My mind has the property of *being capable of existing without my body*.
3. My body does not have the property of being capable of existing without my body.
4. My mind and my body don't have exactly the same properties.

ergo, 5. My mind is not identical to my body.

Notice immediately that this line of reasoning applies not just to my body taken as a whole, but to any part of it, for instance my brain or my central nervous system. (Just reformulate the argument in one or the other of these terms to see why.) If this is right, then Descartes has happened on an astonishing discovery: There's more in the world than just physical objects; in addition there are non-physical things like minds!

To see the significance of this conclusion consider the question, what kinds of thing exist? Well, you'll say, there are everyday objects like tables, chairs, and houses, and there are more esoteric things like quarks, black holes, and electromagnetic forces. Put at the most abstract level, one might say that there are material things—things that are either made of, or are characteristics of, matter. It might seem that this accounts for everything in the universe. Further, it seems incontrovertible that the mind is closely connected with the central nervous system. We know that one can learn a great deal about what is going on in someone's mind by studying such things as MRI scans of his brain. If Descartes were with us right now he would acknowledge this close *connection* between mind and matter. He would, however, deny that this close connection is the same as *identity*. He would point out that nothing in the fascinating field of neuroscience undermines his five-line argument above.

Answers to the question, what kinds of thing exist? start either with a view to the effect that there is one kind of thing, or a view to the effect that there are two kinds of thing. The former types of answer are versions of *monism;* the latter are versions of *dualism*. The form of monism claiming that everything is material is, you guessed it, materialistic monism. (History has also seen defenses of idealistic monism, the view that everything that exists is mental.) Dualism, by contrast, holds that there are two kinds of thing in the world, neither reducible to the other, namely, material things and mental things. If dualism is right, then physics, biology, chemistry, and the other physical sciences cannot give us a complete account of everything that there is; while they can account for a great deal, they cannot give us a full account of the class of nonmaterial things, namely, the world's minds. That's a pretty big gap.

Please note that I am not saying that Descartes' dualism is correct. We aren't ready to decide that question just yet. What I do want to be clear is that (a) a good deal hangs on whether dualism is true or not, and (b) Descartes' dualism is not a perverse or frivolous position. Looking back at the five-line argument above, I'll bet you'll be hard-pressed to find where, if anywhere, it goes wrong. Premises 1, 2, and 3 seem eminently reasonable, and the argument is surely valid. In the last few decades dualism has been lampooned and vilified by many thinkers both within and outside philosophy. What few writers realize, however, is that dualism is supported by an argument that is very powerful indeed. If you're going to reject dualism, you'd better earn the right to do so by making clear where the above argument goes wrong.

La Mettrie and Machines

Ontology is the study of what there is. We may crystallize some major options for ontology with a little tree:

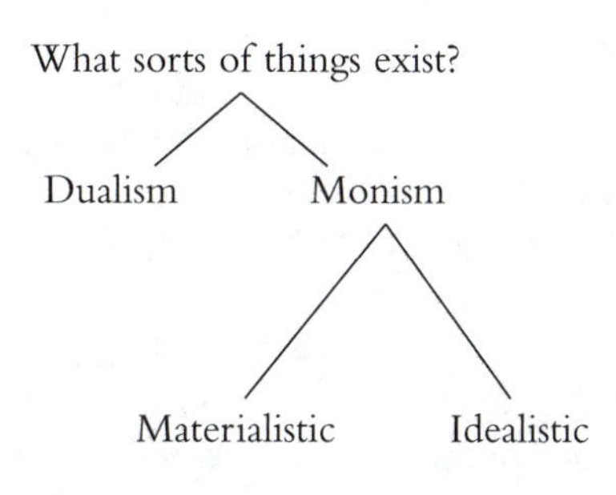

Figure 2: Ontological Options

Many writers subsequent to Descartes wanted to oppose his position with a form of monism. This is not because they took the measure of his argument for that position and figured out where it goes wrong; on the contrary, many writers leave it less than clear whether they really appreciate the power of dualism. At the same time, though, a dualistic ontology raises some vexing questions. For instance, it sure seems that my mind can make changes in the physical world and vice versa. Here I sit with the intention to raise my hand and—zowie!—up goes my hand. And don't forget that orange that caused my experience of the orange. Mind and matter seem to interact all the time. However, if you're a dualist this fact is going to seem bizarre. How can something allegedly nonphysical, like a mind, make a change in something physical, like a hand? One would have thought that the only things that can bring about physical changes are other physical things: pool cues and billiard balls move other billiard balls, the

Himalayas are slowly rising because of continental drift, and so on. Yet dualism seems to deny this. Dualism seems to require that sometimes a physical change, like the moving of my hand, can be brought about by a nonphysical event, like my decision to raise my hand. That's really puzzling.

The French philosopher-physician Julien Offray de La Mettrie (1709–51) wrote at a time when Descartes' dualism was widely accepted in spite of difficulties such as that just mentioned. Dualism at least seemed to explain how we can be free agents in what otherwise seems a deterministic world. (We'll turn to this topic in some detail in Chapter 6.) It also seems to make sense of how, as suggested by themes in the Judeo-Christian tradition, human beings are special in comparison with much of the rest of the material world. Nevertheless, La Mettrie urges,

> Slit open the guts of man and animals. How can you grasp human nature if you never see how the innards of one exactly parallel the innards of the other? (*Man a Machine*, p. 36)

That is, La Mettrie urges us to set aside conceptual analysis and investigate things empirically. When we do so, he tells us, we will find that there is more continuity between human beings and the rest of the animal kingdom than there is discontinuity (Ibid. p. 41). Indeed,

> It is obvious that there is only one substance in the universe and that man is the most perfect animal. Man is to apes and the most intelligent animals what Huygens' planetary pendulum is to a watch of Julien le Roy. If more instruments, wheelwork, and springs are required to show the movements of the planets than to remark and repeat the hours, if Vaucanson needed more art to make his flute player than his duck, he would need even more to make a talker. . . . The human body is an immense clock, constructed with so much artifice and skill that if the wheel that marks the seconds stops because of rust or derailment, the minutes wheel continues turning, as does the quarter hour wheel, and all the rest. (Ibid., p. 69)

One who reads La Mettrie today cannot fail to be struck by, "the Rabelaisian mirth, the cheery collegiality, the infectious enthusiasm, and finally the triumphant defiance, with which La Mettrie puts forward his views," as Justin Leiber has aptly put it. However, it is one thing to claim, as La Mettrie does, that thinking is a material process, and quite another to explain how it is possible for matter to possess cognition, emotion, or experience. This is a particular concern, because we have seen Descartes give a powerful argument—powerful because it assumes so little—on behalf of dualism. If we are to accept a materialistic monism, we should try to understand where Descartes' argument on behalf of dualism goes wrong. In addition, if we are to accept a materialistic monism, we should try to understand what it could possibly mean to say that some hunk of matter is thinking.

Let us approach the latter task first. Suppose someone sits down next to you on the bus and starts to tell you what the rock he is holding in his hand is thinking about. I'm guessing that you'll begin to wonder when your next stop is or if there's an open seat nearby. You'll intuitively feel that it just doesn't make sense to suppose that that rock could be thinking. Rocks aren't in that line of business. However, if you are sympathetic with materialistic monism you'll be of the opinion that some forms of matter are capable of cognition, emotion, or experience. Which forms are they? A natural idea, following La Mettrie's lead, is that they are forms of matter that are more complicated; in particular, they're the forms of matter that are capable of *behaving intelligently*. Unlike the case of a rock, it at least seems to make sense to ask of a mechanical device with which you're having a conversation, whether it's truly intelligent or instead only apparently so. We will develop this line of thought in the next section.

Ryle and the Category Mistake

Not until the 1947 publication of Gilbert Ryle's *The Concept of Mind* do we find the first criticism of Descartes' dualism that also shows where his argument for dualism goes wrong. To understand this criticism, it helps first to understand Ryle's concept of a logical construction: A logical construction is an entity that exists only in the sense of being definable in terms of other entities that are more basic. The average U.S. taxpayer might make $37,405. We know exactly what that means. But notice that when we talk about the average taxpayer we don't expect to be referring to a real person of flesh and blood. Imagine your friend tells you she is going on a biking trip this summer in search of the average taxpayer, and expects to find him somewhere in Nebraska. I suppose you'd politely reply that your friend is mixed up: The average taxpayer is just a construction out of all the real taxpayers that there are, not another flesh and blood citizen in Nebraska or anywhere else.

Ryle tells us that when we fail to recognize an entity is a logical construction, we are committing a *category mistake*. Here is another example: Imagine you're studying for the year at the famed University of Heidelberg and your parents come to visit. You spend the day showing them the classrooms, the lecture halls, the libraries, the dining halls, the students, the professors, and so forth. As the day draws to a close, your father says, "This has been a lovely tour. We've seen the students, the lecture halls, and so forth. But you still haven't shown us the legendary University of Heidelberg. Do we still have time to see that before dinner? Our reservations are for 8 PM." You'll reply to him by pointing out that the University of Heidelberg is those things you've shown him, taken all together. It's nothing over and above all the students, professors, buildings, and the like, working in harmony with one another. To think otherwise is mistakenly to place the idea of a university in the wrong category, for it's a logical construction out of the things you've just spent your day seeing.

Ryle now argues that we are prone to category mistakes about the mind. You might think that the mind is a substance, just as your cyclist friend might think that the average taxpayer is a flesh and blood person. However, Ryle contends that the expression "the mind" really refers to a set of behaviors and dispositions to behavior. To see why, imagine you are trying to learn about a new acquaintance named Montserrat. You find out that she is a good bird spotter, short tempered, a spendthrift, and an excellent listener. What does it mean to be a good bird spotter? Consider an analogy with salt: Salt dissolves in unsaturated water. It is *disposed* to dissolve in a liquid of this kind even when it is in an undissolved state. We can specify this disposition more precisely:

> Salt is soluble just in case it is disposed to dissolve in unsaturated water, which in turn holds just in case, *if* it is placed in unsaturated water, *then* it will dissolve.

I've just given a dispositional account of salt's solubility. Ryle suggests that we can similarly give a dispositional account of many mental characteristics. For instance,

> Montserrat is a good bird spotter just in case she is disposed to detect interesting and unusual birds under difficult observational condition, and this in turn holds just in case, *if* confronted with an interesting or unusual bird under difficult observational conditions, *then* she will discern what kind of bird it is.

Similarly, being short tempered means that Montserrat is disposed to get angry under minimal provocation; being a spendthrift means she is disposed to impulse shopping, and so forth. Ryle suggests that when you come to know a person you learn a huge number of dispositions like these, some momentous, some piddling, and lots in between. Ryle goes even farther in suggesting that a mind just is a huge set of dispositions to behavior of various kinds. For him the mind is *a set of multitrack dispositions to behavior.*

The view that the mind is a set of multitrack dispositions to behavior is a species of what has come to be known as *behaviorism*. Beware: Behaviorism takes many forms. According to the version of behaviorism best known in psychology and associated with figures like James Watson and B. F. Skinner, mental items like beliefs, emotions, and experiences may or not be real, but we should make no appeal to them in a scientific theory of behavior, human or otherwise. This *methodological behaviorism* does not tell us what a mind is and does not try to offer a contribution to ontology. Instead it is a precept for constructing a scientific psychology. By contrast, *reductive behaviorism* argues that the mind is a logical construction out of various states and dispositions of matter. This form of behaviorism tries to support materialistic monism by explaining mental phenomena in purely materialistic terms. Ryle's version of behaviorism is different from both methodological behaviorism and reductive behaviorism. Unlike methodological behaviorism, Ryle does not eschew talk of the mind and mental phenomena. However, unlike reductive behaviorism, Ryle does not try to characterize mental phenomena in purely materialistic terms. For all Ryle knows, mental characteristic such as tenacity or submissiveness might only be explicable in terms of *other* mental characteristics. According to Ryle's version of behaviorism, then, the mind is not a substance, and it is not reducible to one, either. But that doesn't mean the mind is an immaterial substance! Thinking of the mind as a substance that is either material or immaterial belies, Ryle would say, a category mistake in which we fail to see that it is a logical construction out of tendencies to behavior.

Ryle refuses to answer the question whether behavior is itself a material or nonmaterial process and for this reason concludes that a choice between dualism and materialism is bogus. In a moment we will see Ryle getting his comeuppance for this refusal. Until then, let's take stock of his response to Descartes. Ryle is surely right that at least *a lot* of what we take to characterize someone's mind is how they are disposed to behave under various circumstances. Stupid is as stupid does, as they say, and one only learns certain things about someone by seeing what they do in the clutch. A theory that fails to make sense of how what is in our minds disposes us to various kinds of behavior will be impoverished. On the other hand, it is less clear that dispositions to behavior, even a great many of them, tell us *all* there is to know about the mind. There are two reasons for this: First, one might still wish to understand the basis of these dispositions, and, second, one might wonder whether dispositions fully account for the experiential component of the mind. We discuss these two questions in the next three sections.

The Identity Theory

Let's agree that part of what it is to be angry is to be disposed to act in certain characteristic ways (clenching fists, furrowing brow, breaking crockery); likewise for being in pain or for experiencing a smell of vanilla. The trouble is that these dispositions themselves seem to require some explanation. To see why, return to the salt. No chemist worth their salt would suppose that they have given a full account of this substance's behavior by appeal to its tendency to dissolve in unsaturated water. Instead they would explain how its microstructure, in particular its crystalline structure, interacts with water molecules to cause it to dissolve. In giving such an explanation the chemist provides a basis for the disposition of salt to dissolve under certain conditions.

My point is not that citing dispositions is a mistake. It's rather that dispositions are a halfway house on the road to knowledge. A fuller theory will always explain *why* a given object has the dispositions that it does. Matters are not so different in the case of the mind. It is true that anger tends to make us behave in certain characteristic ways, but it is also legitimate to ask why it does that. What is the mechanism by which anger increases blood flow to the arms and often the face, raises the voice, and tends to make us feel something akin to a burning inside? An answer to this question would provide a basis for the behavioral dispositions associated with anger, thereby advancing our knowledge. David Armstrong captures this sentiment nicely with the remark:

> When I think, but my thoughts do not issue in any action, it seems as obvious as anything is obvious that there is something actually going on in me which constitutes my thought. It is not simply that I would speak or act if some conditions that are unfulfilled were to be fulfilled. Something is currently going on, in the strongest and most literal sense of "going on," and this something is my thought. Rylean Behaviorism denies this, and so it is unsatisfactory as a theory of mind. ("The Nature of Mind," in *The Mind/Brain Identity Theory,* ed. C. Borst. London: Macmillan, 1970, pp. 42–61)

Armstrong's point is not that everything Ryle says is untrue; rather it is that Ryle has not gone far enough in explaining how it is possible for matter to be intelligent or, more generally, to possess mental characteristics. Armstrong proffers an answer to this question: He suggests that a mental state is a state of an organism apt for producing a range of behavior, in particular that range of behavior articulated by behaviorists such as Ryle. This state is the source of and explanation of the dispositions mentioned by Ryle.

Armstrong is very clear about the next step in the development of his form of materialistic monism. In specifying a mental state as a state of an organism responsible for a range of behavior, Armstrong understands that this leaves open the question what this state might be. For all we know a priori, it might be an immaterial substance such as that described by Descartes. However, Armstrong offers as an empirical hypothesis that this state is in fact a state of the central nervous system. Armstrong and others make so bold a conjecture as that thinking, emoting, and experiencing are all simply identical with processes in the central nervous system, where those processes are also the source of the dispositions described by Ryle.

Your response might now be: "Of course! What could be more obvious?" It might seem to go nearly without saying that thinking, emoting, and experiencing are just things taking place inside one's head; they are most likely the activation of ensembles of neurons. On this suggestion, thinking about my grandmother is just a matter of the activation of certain neurons; feeling excited about the tennis match

I am watching is likewise just a matter of the activation of a different set of neurons in my central nervous system.

Now, I have a confession: One of the things that drew me to philosophy in college was that in philosophy one can question ideas that seem painfully obvious to nearly everyone else. I remember sitting around a dinner table with friends—budding engineers, economists, lawyers—asking why they felt so sure that mental states are neurological events. After all, other cultures and other epochs have felt that mental states occur elsewhere than the brain, which itself has been taken at various times to be simply a cooling system for the body. To this it is natural to reply: "Well, the evidence is just overwhelmingly in favor of the conclusion that your brain is where thinking and other mental states happen." I would reply to this in turn by saying: Chauvinist!

Not too long ago in Western cultures it was commonly thought that only men are capable of high achievements in the arts and the sciences. We have come to see this as a form of chauvinism, an unjustifiable preference for one group (in this case, men) over another (in this case, women) on the basis of irrelevant characteristics (in this case, genitalia). Racism is another form of chauvinism. So too, one can nowadays hear the charge of chauvinism leveled against those who think that human beings are the only animals with rights: Such people would say that "speciesism" is a form of chauvinism as well. Those who think that mental events are processes in the central nervous system seem to be committed to the view that if you lack gray matter, you can't have mental states. That seems rash at the very least. After all, it sure seems conceivable that we could come across an alien life form that is constructed in an entirely different way from us—perhaps with no neurons at all—and yet seems to show all the signs of mentality. Members of this life form beat our top chess Grand Masters, write excellent poetry and compose beautiful symphonies, and their scientific theories are more powerful than our own. It seems chauvinistic to hold that because they lack grey matter, they can't *really* have mental states. At the very least, it seems a mistake to let a philosophical theory, such as Armstrong's, decide this issue a priori rather than allowing us to investigate the situation more carefully to draw our own conclusions. La Mettrie had a point!

Minds and Computers

Dualism seems unsatisfactory, and behaviorism incomplete at best, while materialistic monism appears chauvinistic. How can we proceed? In response to difficulties like those we just encountered in

Armstrong's version of monism, it might be suggested that we consider a simple machine. A lever, for instance, is any object that has a fulcrum, can bear a load, and can have work applied to it. A wheelbarrow, a seesaw, even your arm are all forms of levers. Notice that in defining a lever I said nothing about what it has to be made of. Granted, you won't get far trying to make a seesaw out of butter at room temperature. On the other hand, so long as you use something fairly rigid it doesn't matter what you choose: it can be wood, steel, granite, plastic, and so on. One might say that the lever is *multiply realizable:* the description we have given of the lever can be realized, within limits, in a variety of material forms.

What we have said about levers suggests a way out of our chauvinism problem about minds. Granted, minds are not as easy to define as levers. However, if a mental state can be characterized, at least in part, in terms of dispositions to behavior, then it might be suggested that any such state is that disposition plus *some* physical realization or other. Just as it doesn't much matter what a lever is made of so long as it can do the job, so, too, on this approach it doesn't much matter how a mental state is realized so long as it disposes its owner to behave in the relevant way. Clusters of neurons give one way in which the mental state might be realized, but that state might instead be realized in, for instance, silicon chips.

This is the doctrine of *functionalism*. The functionalist holds that a mental state M is a state of an entity (not necessarily an organism) produced by characteristic environmental stimuli, and in conjunction with other mental states, M tends to produce characteristic behavioral output. Functionalists typically add the further proviso that those states take some physical form or other. That is, while, strictly speaking, one can be a functionalist without requiring that the functional state in question be physical, most functionalists offer their position as an improvement on all the theories we have canvassed so far, and most hold that requiring a *physical* realization is necessary to achieve this gain. Let's follow the majority of thinkers in this choice.

Functionalism has its virtues. For one, it's not chauvinistic. It leaves open the possibility that in principle there may be a creature with a radically different internal structure from our own but which nevertheless possesses cognitive, affective, or experiential states. In fact, functionalism doesn't even require that mental states be realized in living creatures; for all we have said so far, a computer could realize a functional organization of a sort to give it a mind. Second, it improves upon Ryle's form of behaviorism by offering a physical basis for the dispositions that he adduces in explaining mentality. In this way functionalism seems to combine the good things about Ryle's behaviorism and the identity theory, while eschewing the bad.

Another nice thing about functionalism is that it raises the fascinating question whether computers could think, feel, or experience. In fact, functionalism is committed to the view that if a computer has the right sort of functional organization, it would be able to do all of these things. Some will find this implication welcome; others will find it so ghastly as to refute the theory that implies it. Let's tread carefully here. First, to those who find the prospect of a "thinking machine" disturbing, let's be clear on whether this response is relevant. Many possible theories or findings might be disturbing. I would find it disturbing to learn that certain racial groups have characteristically higher or lower intelligence than those of the general population. Yet the fact that this might be disturbing would do nothing to refute the finding. Similarly, if functionalism implies that machines (if only those that are beyond our current technological limitations) can think, and that seems disturbing to you, then that is no skin off the back of functionalism. The functionalist might just reply: "Welcome to the desert of the real."

Second, one could point out that there could not be a thinking machine because any "intelligence" it possesses would have to have been placed there by the engineers and programmers who built it. This, however, does not seem to be a feature that distinguishes machines from us. After all, our genetic make up and environment (including the influence of our teachers and parents) have fed a great deal of information into our minds over a long period of time. That fact doesn't seem to threaten our right to be called thinking things; nor should such a fact threaten the right of computers to this nomination.

Third, one could object that no machine could achieve the kind of creativity necessary for composing a great symphony, discovering a cure for a disease, painting a beautiful picture, proving a profound mathematical theorem, etc. This claim is, however, questionable on two grounds: First of all, plenty of us are entirely bereft of creative ability. Many people simply lack the capacity for these feats. Yet I doubt that one who makes this third objection really believes that those human beings who are not at all creative don't really have minds. Furthermore, computers these days can do some pretty impressive things. Chess-playing computers can modify their programs to take into account the strategic personalities of their opponents. In addition, there are mathematical theorems that have only been possible to prove with the aid of computers. I likewise see no bar in principle to the possibility of a computer composing some wonderful music; for all I know it has already been done.

The 1980s and 1990s witnessed a raging controversy over the question whether computers can think. Proponents of so-called artificial intelligence contended that it is possible in principle for computers to think; their opponents were resourceful in suggesting things that computers cannot do. Now that the dust has begun to settle we can see that much of the controversy revolved around the experiential component of the mind. It is not at all clear what it would be for a computer to experience pain or for it to have a sensation of yellow. Of course, one might hold that a computer can be possessed of cognition without having experiences as well. We need not get sidetracked with that issue, for the experiential component of the mind raises some of the most pressing philosophical questions of our day.

Consciousness

Functionalism goes a long way in accounting for many mental states that are associated with characteristic patterns of behavior. It seems an improvement over La Mettrie's materialism, over Ryle's behaviorism, and over Armstrong's identity theory. However, some mental states are not associated with any such patterns of behavior, and others that are so associated contain elements that still seem to be left untouched by a functional characterization. Consider a sensation such as I have when I look at something yellow in good light under normal perceptual conditions. This sensation tends to be caused by my retina receiving light at a certain wavelength. It might also, in conjunction with other mental states, tend to produce characteristic behavior such as my uttering words like "yellow" if I am an English speaker. But this functional characterization of an experience of yellow doesn't seem fully to capture what is going on when I have that experience, because there is a distinctive quality to the experience of yellow, a quality that no other experience quite has and that doesn't seem to manifest itself in my tendencies to behavior.

To grasp this point more vividly, imagine that the aliens that we mentioned earlier appear on Earth one day. They are extremely good investigators, and in little time they figure out the functional organization of human beings. However, imagine also that these aliens have sensory systems radically different from our own. They lack eyes, but instead use sonar to echolocate their way around. In addition, they can often find things that are hidden to our own eyes because they have organs much like the ampullae of Lorenzini found in many species of shark, organs that enable them to detect electrical activity in living organisms and elsewhere. Sonar and the ampullae of Lorenzini are apparently the aliens' only sensory organs; they lack smell, vision, hearing, touch, and taste. (As it happens, we don't know whether they have proprioception.)

Consider the consequences of the aliens' limited sensory capacity. They have no idea what the yellowness of a lemon looks like. They have not the faintest clue of the smell of vanilla, or the sound of a trumpet. As a result, in spite of knowing the full functional organization of human minds, they know very little about how the world appears from our point of view. More generally, while the aliens might know everything there is to know about our physical makeup and functional organization, they are clueless as to what yellow lemons look like, how trumpets sound, and so forth. Because of that, they seem to lack a complete understanding of our minds. (Of course, we are in a symmetrical situation with respect to them; we have no idea what it would feel like to experience a thing through electroreception, and even a full neurophysiological description of alien brains won't help us to get that knowledge.)

We are now face-to-face with one version of the *problem of consciousness:* Very broadly, the problem of consciousness strives to make sense of the possibility of conscious experience in a purely physical world. The case of the aliens makes vivid the fact that one can know all there is to know on the physical level without knowing what is going on at the experiential level. Yet an ability to get experiential knowledge out of physical information seems to be required if we are to understand the physical basis of consciousness. After all, it is one thing to say that having a central nervous system or some other suitable physical realization is necessary for experience; it is quite another thing to say that adverting to what happens on the physical level can account for the nature of that experience. This latter is a stronger claim than the former, and the case of the aliens seems to show that the stronger claim is not true. They know all about us on the physical level yet know very little about what our experiences are like.

The problem of consciousness is not just a challenge to functionalism, it is a challenge to the very idea that the world can be fully understood in physical terms. Naturally, a dualist such as Descartes would, if he were alive today, smirkingly point out that he told us so; perhaps we should never have taken materialistic monism seriously in the first place. On the other hand, as we have seen, dualism raises some mysteries of its own. Further, perhaps we can wriggle out of the problem of consciousness by suggesting that knowing such things as what a lemon looks like or what a trumpet sounds like are abilities rather than states of knowledge. After all, no reasonable person would criticize a physical account of how a bicycle works by complaining that we can know everything there is to know about how a bicycle works without knowing how to ride it. Knowing how to ride a bike is a skill, and if I lack this skill while still knowing the physics of bicycles I can't lay this failing at the door of physics.

A parallel line of reasoning might apply to experience. I know what lemons look like and how trumpets sound. I can manifest these bits of knowledge by calling up the look or sound in imagination. Barring that, I can manifest these bits of knowledge by showing that I can tell the lemon looks and the trumpet sounds from all the other experiences I might have. (If you have doubts about whether I know what a trumpet sounds like, present me with the sound of each wind instrument in an orchestra to see if I can detect the trumpet.) However, all these ways of manifesting knowledge boil down to abilities that I might possess. I am *able* to tell the lemon looks from the strawberry looks and the tomato looks; I am *able* to discriminate the trumpet sounds from the oboe sounds and piccolo sounds. If that is right, then knowing what an experience feels like is more like being able to ride a bicycle than knowing a bit of factual information.

This *ability hypothesis* (knowing what an experience is like is an ability, not a matter of possessing a piece of factual information) has come under heavy fire among students of consciousness, and some have gone so far as to hold that the very phenomenon of consciousness shows that a purely physical explanation of the world is impossible. Those who hold this pessimistic opinion don't, in general, do so for the perverse pleasure of gainsaying the possibility of a purely scientific explanation of our world. Instead, many come to that conclusion reluctantly. Before reaching that drastic conclusion, however, I would suggest that we do well to be very clear about just what a physical explanation of the mind should give us. That question is a topic of current discussion among philosophers, neuroscientists, and psychologists.

Study Questions

1. In the first two of his *Meditations,* Descartes considers the possibility that all of his beliefs are false. First, how do (a) illusions, (b) hallucinations, and (c) dreams sometimes bring about false beliefs in us? Next, even if Descartes can somehow rule out the possibility that he is dreaming, what further, more troublesome, possibility would he have to rule out in order to be confident in even such apparently obvious beliefs as that he has a pair of hands?

2. Descartes argues that even if he cannot rule out this more troublesome possibility, there is a first proposition about which he cannot be mistaken. What is the first proposition about which he believes he cannot be mistaken, and how does he show that he cannot be mistaken about it?

3. Suppose you have a "second-order" belief about the contents of your own mind, such as a belief that might be expressed with the words, "I seem to see an apple before me." (A "first-order" belief would be expressed as "There is an apple before me.") Would that belief turn out to be wrong if, in fact, you are dreaming? Please explain your answer.

4. Please explain the indiscernibility of identicals. Next, Descartes holds that his essence consists entirely in his being a thinking thing (*Meditations,* p. 51). He seems to infer from this that it is in principle possible for his mind to exist without his body, indeed without his brain. Please explain how Descartes concludes from this observation that his mind and body are in fact distinct.

5. La Mettrie opposes Descartes' dualism with a form of materialistic monism. How does he justify that position? How might Descartes respond to that attempted justification?

6. Explain what it is to commit a category mistake as Ryle construes that notion. Next, give a relatively simple example of a category mistake. Why would Ryle charge Descartes with committing a category mistake? In your answer, please be sure to explain Ryle's view that mental characteristics like "irritated" and "elated" refer to behavior and/or dispositions to behavior.

7. Armstrong agrees with Ryle in holding that mental characteristics may be defined in part in terms of behavior and dispositions to behavior. Why would Armstrong nevertheless charge Ryle with failing to take a necessary further step, namely, assigning a "categorical" basis to these dispositions? (In your answer it will be helpful to draw on analogy with dispositional properties of inorganic substances such as salt or glass.) Finally, after formulating this objection to Ryle, at what position concerning the relation between mind and body does Armstrong arrive?

8. Suppose one defines mental properties such as being angry or thinking about Toledo, as states of the central nervous system disposed to produce various kinds of characteristic behavior. Why might a position of this sort seem liable to a charge of chauvinism?

9. How does functionalism offer a theory of the mind that does not seem to succumb to the charge of chauvinism? Functionalism seems to imply that it is possible in principle for computers to think. Does that refute the theory? Why or why not?

10. Consciousness seems to be particularly difficult to explain in materialistic terms. Please explain why this is so.

Suggestions for Further Reading

Plato. *Republic,* translated by C.D.C. Reeve, 2nd edition. Indianapolis: Hackett Publishing Company, 1992.

Descartes. *Meditations on First Philosophy,* translated by D. A. Cress. Indianapolis: Hackett Publishing Company, 1993.

La Mettrie, Julien Offray de. *Man a Machine*, ed. Justin Lieber. Indianapolis: Hackett Publishing Company, 1994.

Ryle, G. *The Concept of Mind.* Chicago: University of Chicago Press, 1984.

Rosenthal, D. *Materialism and the Mind–Body Problem,* 2nd edition. Indianapolis: Hackett Publishing Company, 2000.

Lycan, W. *Mind and Cognition: A Reader.* Oxford: Blackwell, 1990.

Heil, J. *The Philosophy of Mind.* New York: Routledge, 2004.

Wilson, T. D. *Strangers to Ourselves: Discovering the Adaptive Unconscious.* Cambridge: Harvard University Press, 2002.

Turing, A. "Computing Machinery and Intelligence." *Mind,* vol. 59 (1950), pp. 433–60.

Hodges, A. *Alan Turing: The Enigma.* New York: Simon and Schuster, 1983.

Irwin, W., ed. *The Matrix and Philosophy: Welcome to the Desert of the Real.* La Salle: Open Court, 2002.

———. *More Matrix and Philosophy: Revolutions and Reloaded Decoded.* La Salle: Open Court, 2005.

Haugeland, J. *Artificial Intelligence: The Very Idea.* Cambridge, MA: MIT Press.

Cunningham, S. *What Is a Mind?* Indianapolis: Hackett Publishing Company, 2000.

Movies Significant for the Philosophy of Mind

The Matrix (1999), directed by Andy and Larry Wachowski.

The Matrix Reloaded (2003), directed by Andy and Larry Wachowski.

Waking Life (2001), directed by Richard Linklater.

6. Are You Free?

Here are some things you probably think of as being up to you: Whether to put on brown or blue socks in the morning, what to have for dinner, how to spend your weekend, what career path to follow. Not everyone has a choice in such matters. Some people have no choice at all about what to have for dinner: it's either rice or starvation. Likewise, a person might be forced to pursue one line of work under threat of torture or death, but even if that is true then she still probably has some choice in other matters. Not that it's much consolation, but she might still have some say in whether she chooses to scratch her nose now or two minutes from now. These cases involve *freedom of action,* the ability freely to choose whether to perform one action rather than another.

Philosophers wonder about this notion of freedom of action, and about whether we genuinely have it. In addition, philosophers concern themselves with a slightly more abstract kind of freedom, freedom of will. Consider the set of desires that you have for this that or another thing: An orange, a new car, a career in medicine, even world peace. Some of these desires, if they are genuine and not just idle fantasy, will tend to produce consequences in your behavior. The desire for an orange will bring you to choose an orange if one is available at lunch, the desire for the car will bring you to save up for one, and so forth. Let us call all those desires that are at least partly effective in bringing you to act in pursuit of a goal your *will.*

You might not be happy with every aspect of your will. I wish I didn't like cake as much as I do. If I didn't like it so much I could probably drop a few pounds, and that would make things easier on my knees when I am running. But there you can find me, again and again polishing off more than my share. This cake liking is an aspect of my will that I would like to change. Or your will might include the desire to compete with others at every opportunity. You are always looking for opponents in board games, debates, sports, clothing, and so on. You might also get to the point in your life at which you feel that somehow all this energy is misspent. "Why," you might ask yourself, "do I feel the need to be competing constantly when maybe if I give people a chance they might like me for other reasons than my prowess as an opponent?"You might also begin to feel as if you would like to try to change this aspect of your will. Maybe over time you can start to be more interested in *learning* from conversations and less interested in *winning* them. If you feel this way, then you, too, have found an aspect of your will that you'd like to change.

Not all aspects of our will are things that we can change. Someone who is agoraphobic, chronically and intensely afraid of crowds, might be this way simply because of her genetic inheritance. She might be unable to change her agoraphobia. Perhaps the most she can hope for is to manage it by staying away from crowds whenever possible. If so, then there is an aspect of her will that is not free. She is not free to have the will she would choose to have on issues concerning going out in public. Other aspects of our will do seem to be under our control. I am confident that with enough concentration on the ill-health effects of being overweight, including adult-onset diabetes and heart disease, together with just staying away from bakeries and the cake table at parties, I can lose or at least decrease my strong desire for cake. Not only do I have freedom of choice on the matter of whether to eat this third piece in front of me, I also have freedom of will on the matter of whether to be a cake fiend in the first place. Thus in addition to freedom of action, the ability freely to choose whether to perform one action rather than another, is *freedom of will,* the ability to choose whether to have one kind of will rather than another. The so-called "free will problem" in philosophy really includes both freedom of action and freedom of will, and while the majority of discussion historically has been on the topic of freedom of action, we will be concerned with both freedom of action and freedom of will in this chapter.

Universal Determinism and Its Challenge to Freedom

Modern physics as we know it began its spectacular rise in 17th-century Europe, inspired by, among others, the epoch-making work of Isaac Newton. Newton's *Principia* showed that we can account for the motion of a cannonball through the air to its target, as well as the orbits of planets around the Sun, in rigorous mathematical terms. If we can get the mathematics right, then nothing will be left up to chance. In particular, scientists saw that if we can get an accurate description of the laws of motion and of the quantities characterizing a given object—its mass, position, etc.—we can give a full account of how it will behave as other objects and forces act upon it. Indeed, both physicists and philosophers (in fact, in those days, one person could wear both hats) began to speculate that perhaps all of nature is governed by deterministic laws. Not just the orbit of planets around the Sun and the movements of billiard balls on a billiards table, but all things, perhaps, are governed by laws that fully account for their behavior.

This idea may be expressed in the thesis known as *universal determinism:*

> Every material event that occurs in the history of the universe has a prior and sufficient material condition.

We might not know those sufficient conditions, and we surely can't keep track of more than a very few events in the universe. However, universal determinism (UD for short) says that there is some prior and sufficient material condition for every event that occurs, be it something awe-inspiring like the explosion of a supernova, or something so lowly as the settling of a piece of dust on your pillow.

Consider the implications of UD. If UD is true, then the settling of that piece of dust on your pillow is something that had a prior sufficient material condition, which *itself* had a prior sufficient condition, which *itself* had a prior sufficient condition, and so on for a very long way back, presumably to the big bang. If this is correct, then the settling of that piece of dust on your pillow is something that could in principle have been predicted hours before by a computer with enough information and processing power—in fact, days before; in fact, come to think of it, millennia before! The computer would have to be very big and very fast to deal with all the needed parameters, but in principle if UD is true then a machine could make such a prediction with perfect accuracy. The French mathematician-physicist Laplace put this point eloquently in 1825:

> We ought . . . to consider the present state of the universe as the effect of its previous state and as the cause of that which is to follow. An intelligence that, at a given instant, could comprehend all the forces by which nature is animated and the respective situations of the beings that make it up, if moreover it were vast enough to submit these data to analysis, would encompass in the same formula the movements of the greatest bodies of the universe and those of the lightest atoms. For such an intelligence nothing would be uncertain, and the future,

> like the past, would be open to its eyes. (*Philosophical Essay on Probabilities,* pp. 2–3)

The intelligence that Laplace refers to might be a machine or a conscious creature of some kind; it doesn't make any difference for the present question.

So what? Well, let's suppose for a moment that monistic materialism is true, so that the only things that exist are material objects as well as forces that govern those objects. That of course will include you: If materialistic monism is true, then you are just a material object as well. But in that case, all of the events having to do with you are under the sway of universal determinism as well. So now switch the example from a speck of dust settling on your pillow to your reaching for and grabbing an orange one day in a cafeteria at lunch. That orange-grab—call it E_1—was caused by a cascade of neural and muscular events originating in your brain; these events are presumably the sufficient condition required by UD. Call this set of events E_2. If UD holds, then E_2 will in turn have a prior and sufficient material condition, namely some event or set of events E_3. And so on, back as far as we care to trace the etiology of E_3.

We may see now that if UD is true, then your orange-grab, E_1, is something that in principle could have been predicted hours, days, years before it happened, in fact even before you were born. Of course, I chose the example of the orange-grab pretty much at random. These same points apply to more momentous examples like what college you choose, whom you choose as your friends or spouse, what career to pursue, etc. If UD is true, then all these things could in principle have been predicted by a powerful enough computer even before you were born. This is not to say that these events *were* predicted, but just that they *could* have been.

Many people are willing to accept that our range of choice might be smaller than it appears at first glance. For instance, many children are born into grinding poverty, with violence, drugs, broken homes, abuse, and neglect a part of their daily lives. By the time such a child is a teenager, the idea that she could break out of the cycle and make something of herself seems hardly realistic. Again, every new science supplement to a major newspaper seems to report just-discovered genetic influences on our behavior: on our musical talent, on our ability to empathize with others, on our tendency to be overweight, and so on. A great deal of what widely accepted opinion twenty, thirty, or forty years ago might have said is subject to our free choice now seems to be heavily influenced by our genetic inheritance plus our environmental influences.

In spite of all these ways in which scientific investigation has narrowed the scope of free will, it nevertheless seems that in some cases we still truly have a choice. To put the point in the terminology of the last section, it seems that in some cases we have freedom of action. There you are, deliberating between the orange and the apple. It sure *feels* like you can decide which it is going to be. There you are, struggling with the question whether you are going to keep the promise you made to your friend to keep her secret. Here too it sure *feels* like you can decide whether to keep that secret or get some guaranteed laughs from other friends by spilling it. However, if UD is true, what you end up doing was causally determined by events that had occurred even before you were born—in fact, by events occurring thousands of years ago. Many have concluded that if UD is true, then freedom of action is just an illusion: our actions are no more free than the dust or the planets. Those who conclude this are assuming a thesis known as *incompatibilism:*

> Freedom of action and universal determinism are not compatible with one another.

Incompatibilism says that there isn't enough room in the world for both freedom of action and UD; it does not by itself tell us which one has to go. As we'll see later in this chapter, some incompatibilists reject freedom of action to keep UD; others reject UD to keep freedom of action. I should also make clear once again that UD doesn't mean that some entity does in fact predict your actions before they occur. It only means that such actions could in principle be predicted, for instance, by Laplace's imagined intelligence. Again, if God (defined as the GCB in Chapter 3) exists, then that might mean that God knows every action you are going to perform before you perform it.[1] This phenomenon might seem to some people to raise a problem for free will as well, but if it does raise a problem, it is a different problem from the

[1] Not everyone thinks this follows. For instance, some medieval philosophers thought that the future is genuinely open in such a way that there is truly no fact of the matter about what actions you will perform in the future until you perform them. On that view, even an omniscient being won't know what the future holds.

one raised by UD. The reason is that God's (or for that matter anyone else's) foreknowledge of your action doesn't imply that that action has a prior sufficient material condition. On most views of God's nature, God is not, or not exclusively, a material being. For this reason, God can know beforehand what you are going to do without that implying that there are any material sufficient conditions of your behavior.

You might simply respond to these questions by denying that materialism is true. Perhaps my choosing the orange is not a material event, but rather an event that is at least in part an event in my mind. Those who follow Descartes in holding that our minds are not material substances will tend to offer this response to the challenge that UD seems to raise for the possibility of freedom of action. If you are tempted by this response to the problem raised by UD, then it might be helpful at this point to read or review Chapter 5 to make sure you are clear on some problems with dualism.

Does Quantum Mechanics Save Freedom?

Another response to the challenge raised by universal determinism for freedom of action is to point out that physics in the 20th century rejected it, and the 21st century has not by any means taken it back. Laplace, whom we mentioned in the last section, believed, along with most other experts of his day, that probability is a tool that provides guidance through the world for creatures of limited intelligence and knowledge such as ourselves. On his view, an omniscient being would have no need for the notion of probability, for such a being would be able to calculate every event that did occur, is occurring, or will occur.

Laplace espouses a position that was dominant until the early part of the 20th century. However, the revolutionary work of Max Planck, Werner Heisenberg, Niels Bohr, and others who have built on their findings have convinced much of the scientific community that the world is not deterministic. For instance, take a uranium atom such as U238. According to our best physical theory of these matters, known as quantum mechanics, the U238 atom is liable to lose an electron at some point in its existence. However, our best physical theory only posits a probability space in which that event will occur. Our best theory rules out the possibility that we can predict exactly when that atom will decay in this way; the most we can know is its likelihood of decaying within a certain interval of time. This is a matter of principle rather than our own technological limitations: Quantum mechanics tells us that the atom's decaying at one moment rather than another is not something that has a physical cause. The only thing that has a physical cause is the atom's decaying *within a certain interval.* When exactly the atom decays is irreducibly a matter of chance.

So UD is not true, at least at the subatomic level. Not only that, but we know from the mathematical field of catastrophe theory that subatomic events can wring astonishing changes on the macrocosmic scale. A subatomic event in one place in the Earth's atmosphere might produce a cascade of effects that culminate in a hurricane thousands of miles away!

I don't want for a moment to downplay the importance of quantum indeterminacy or catastrophe theory. What I do want to argue is that if you lack freedom of action in a world governed by universal determinism, you aren't going to get it by moving to a world of quantum indeterminacy.

Why is that? Imagine that what caused your grabbing the orange one day at lunch was a set of neural events that were caused, along the lines of UD, by some prior set of neural events. Now compare this situation with one in which the neural events that bring about your orange-grab are themselves indeterministic, that is, they are not caused by anything when they occur. They occur in a way that is irreducibly a matter of chance, just as with the decay of that uranium atom. How would this latter situation make your orange-grab any more a free action than it would be in a world governed by UD? Richard Taylor puts this idea vividly when he writes,

> This is no description of free, voluntary, or responsible behavior. Indeed, so far as the motions of my body or its parts are entirely uncaused, such motions cannot even be ascribed to me as my behavior in the first place, since I have nothing to do with them. The behavior of my arm is just the random motion of a foreign object. Behavior that is mine must be behavior that is within my control, but motions that occur from no causes are without the control of anyone. I can have no more to do with, and no more control over, the uncaused motions of my limbs than a gambler has over the motions of an honest roulette wheel. I can only, like him, idly wait to see what happens. (Taylor, *Metaphysics,* p. 43)

Taylor's point is that if some of my actions are caused by events that are themselves indeterministic, then they won't be any more up to me than if they were caused by events that follow deterministically from events that occurred before I was born. If breaking the chains of determinism is to make us free, it won't be with the help of quantum mechanics. Accordingly it doesn't seem that quantum mechanics is going to help us overcome the problem raised by UD for freedom of action.

Hume's Compatibilism

According to one tradition in philosophy, some of the perennial problems of the field are due to a failure to define our terms properly. The 18th-century Scottish philosopher, David Hume, whom we encountered earlier in Chapter 3 in our discussion of rational grounds for religious belief, thought that the whole problem of free will rests on a simple failure to clarify what we mean by such expressions as "free will" and "could have done otherwise." Consequently, he felt, the so-called problem of free will is simply a symptom of the bewitchment of our intellect by language. To see why Hume takes this position, note first of all that it is pretty widely agreed that freedom of action is a matter of being able to do otherwise than you do. More precisely,

> Thesis 1. *x freely performs action a* if and only if x performs action a and x could have done otherwise than perform action a.

According to this characterization, freely performing an action is a matter of meeting two conditions, namely, performing the action and being capable of doing otherwise than perform that action. Both these conditions have to be met in order for your action to be free. Thus, if you perform an action, but couldn't help doing so, you didn't perform that action freely. For instance, imagine I eat something at lunch that causes me to go into a seizure in the glassware section of a department store. In the course of that seizure I will probably break some things. However, while I do cause the damage, I can't help it. Even if I had been trying my best not to shatter that charming glass elephant, I might do so all the same. That comports with our thesis 1 above, for it tells us that in such a case, although I did do the damage, I couldn't have done otherwise, and so was not free. Thesis 1 seems pretty reasonable.

Thesis 1 is reasonable, but you might still find it a bit airy. What does this notion of "could have done otherwise" amount to? For some guidance, let's now recall what we learned about dispositions from Ryle in Chapter 5. Salt's solubility is a matter of its having a disposition to dissolve in an unsaturated liquid. This disposition may in turn be explained in terms of a conditional statement:

> *If* this piece of salt is placed in an unsaturated liquid, *then* it will dissolve.

Hume now offers a striking idea. It is that the expression "could have done otherwise" is a veiled dispositional statement, definable in the following terms:

> Thesis 2. *x could have done otherwise than perform action a* if and only if: *if* x were to have chosen to do otherwise, *then* x would have done otherwise than perform action a.

To see why this is a fairly plausible way of understanding what it means to say that someone could have done otherwise than do what she did, let's return to my issues with cake. Suppose you take me to task for eating the piece of cake that had been set aside for you. Surely, you suggest, I could have held back rather than stuffing my face. I reply, "Well, look, that piece of Black Forest cake was simply *howling* my name. I really couldn't resist." You will probably want to reply with something like: "Nice try. But if you had really wanted to exercise self-control, you could have refrained from pigging out." This is just a way of saying that "could have done otherwise" means something quite close to the dispositional notion exhibited above. The suggestion, then, is that "could have" denotes a capacity in me, just as "soluble" denotes a capacity in the salt. I have the capacity to refrain from scarfing down your piece of cake, whereas I don't have the capacity to keep from damaging glassware if I am having a seizure in a department store.

Consider now the implications of this. If we know that A is true if and only if B, and B is true if and only if C, then we may infer that A is true if and only if C. Accordingly, statements (1) and (2) together imply Hume's dispositional analysis of freedom:

> Thesis 3. *x freely performs action a* if and only if x performs action a and *if* x were to have chosen to do otherwise, *then* x would have done otherwise than perform action a.

Now here's the rub. The second half of Hume's dispositional analysis, the part after "if and only if," can be true in a wholly deterministic world! To see why, compare the second half of Thesis 3 with the example of a billiard ball on a billiards table. Suppose it is the eight ball, hit smack into the corner pocket. Imagine also that the billiards table and everything on it make up a wholly deterministic system, so that every material event that occurs on that table has a prior sufficient material condition. Then even though the eight ball goes into the corner pocket, it is still true that if it had been hit differently, it would have gone into another pocket, or no pocket at all. The billiard ball can have a capacity to move differently from the way it does even in a deterministic world.

Similarly, if, in spite of being in a deterministic world, I have the capacity to do differently from what I actually do, then Thesis 3 tells us that I can be free in a deterministic world. This is to say that if Hume's reasoning is correct, then freedom of action can occur in a world in which UD is true. That is why Hume espouses the doctrine of

> *Compatibilism:* Freedom of action and universal determinism are compatible.

Hume doesn't just assert compatibilism; as we have just seen he also argues for it. Accordingly, even though the doctrine of compatibilism might come as a surprise, you need to scrutinize it with some care. It is a bit subtle, and you might need to think it through more than once before it sinks in. After all, if Hume is right, then the whole venerable problem of freedom of action is just a teapot tempest born of a failure to clarify our terms!

Libertarian Critiques of Hume

Hume's attempt to solve the problem of freedom of action by *dissolving* it certainly has its charms. However, although Hume's compatibilist position has had many followers, it has also come in for some heavy criticism. We need not challenge the claim that freedom of action is a matter of having the ability to do otherwise than you do. What has instead come in for criticism is Hume's dispositional analysis, Thesis 3. The trouble is that with some ingenuity one can imagine a situation in which a person could have done otherwise than she does, yet still is not free. The same Taylor whom we met in the discussion of quantum indeterminacy has thought of just such a case.

Taylor asks us to imagine a diabolical neuroscientist who can stimulate various parts of your brain by radio transmission. (In a later section we are going to see that this hypothetical case is not so far-fetched.) He pushes one set of buttons, and you form the intention to grab the orange that is before you; he pushes another set of buttons, and you form the intention to kiss the nearest dog on the nose. These intentions aren't just minor urges, either; they're powerful enough to make you act on them unless some external physical force gets in your way. Now consider the dog-kissing intention: Suppose it results in your smooching a nearby St. Bernard, slobber and all. It sure seems that you aren't a free agent when you do that, any more than you would be if you kissed the dog as a result of a Tourette's syndrome episode. However, it is still true that had you chosen to do otherwise, you would have done otherwise. For instance, Taylor's neuroscientist might have pushed different buttons and stimulated different parts of your brain to make you intend and then attempt to kiss the nearest police officer. In that case, you would have done otherwise than kiss the St. Bernard. But so what? In neither case would you have been free.

The point of this example is that Hume's dispositional analysis of freedom seems doubtful. In particular, it appears that Thesis 3's right side (the counteractual part) can be true without the left side (the being-free part) being true. The person whose brain is being stimulated by the neuroscientist, for instance, satisfies the could-have-done-otherwise part, but nevertheless does not seem free. So the two sides of the dispositional analysis are not equivalent, and so the entire statement does not seem correct. Yet Thesis 3 was a crucial linchpin for Hume's compatibilist project. As a result, his compatibilist project seems to be in trouble.

Taylor sees this as the death of compatibilism. Instead he espouses a form of incompatibilism known as libertarianism. The libertarian holds that in at least some situations you can be sure that you are performing a free action. Consider again that situation in which you are deciding whether to adhere to that promise to keep your friend's secret. You weigh the importance of integrity against the attraction of getting some laughs from the other friends who are with you right now eating lunch. It *is* kind of tempting. Suppose further that after some struggle you resolve to keep that promise after all: Lunch is not as fun as it might have been, but at least you've been true to your friend. The libertarian holds that in this situation the only thing that causes your action of refraining from breaking the promise is your decision to do so. Yet that *decision* is not itself caused by anything either within you or outside of you. Accordingly, that decision to keep the promise is an event, but it is not an event that has a prior sufficient material condition. Some libertarians use the term "agent-causality" to refer to cases of this kind: When an action of mine is brought about by agent-causality, it is caused by me, but its being caused by me is not something that itself has a prior sufficient material condition. The buck stops with me.

To clarify her position the libertarian now needs to make a choice about the status of those decisions. Such a decision is either itself a material event, or, if one is sympathetic with dualism, perhaps instead it is a nonmaterial event. If it is a material event, then we will have a material event that lacks a prior sufficient material condition. If that is so, then it follows that UD, universal determinism, cannot be true. Hence if the libertarian opts for materialism, then she will have to deny that UD is true. Another option, by contrast, is to hold that these decisions are nonmaterial. On this dualist version of libertarianism, the theorist may adhere to UD but pays the price of inheriting the problems that beset dualism generally. We discussed these problems in Chapter 5.

Consider the materialist form of libertarianism. (For the rest of this chapter I will restrict my discussion to this form of the theory.) It has to deny UD. How could a philosopher have the temerity to reject this thesis which, leaving aside quantum indeterminacy, is so well supported by empirical evidence? A philosopher might reply that her denial of UD is based on empirical evidence too, but empirical evidence of a kind that is more secure and immediate than any evidence that we might have for UD. What could that evidence be? Introspection!

Return to the case in which you were deliberating about whether to keep your friend's secret. You can, the libertarian will suggest, look inside yourself and observe yourself choosing what to do with the same certainty you have when you know whether you're in pain or whether something on your tongue tastes sweet. (Recall that we introduced the notion of introspection during our discussion of Descartes in Chapter 5.) In all three of these cases you know simply by introspection what is happening. However, it might be said, introspection is the most secure and reliable form of empirical knowledge;

our knowledge of such things as causal relations among objects outside of us is comparatively indirect and comparatively shaky. For this reason, one might suggest that we *can* gain introspective certainty of a fact that overturns something as empirically well established as UD.

Please let this sink in for a moment. If the materialist libertarian is correct, then we can know by introspection and some simple logical deduction that not every material event has a prior and sufficient material cause. Those that involve the exercise of my will are a case in point. Of course, if we are to be confident that this is a *sound* line of reasoning, in which the argument is not only valid but the premises are also true, then we had better be sure that introspection justifies the confidence that we are taking it to justify. In fact we will see reasons for doubting whether we are really entitled to that confidence.

Hard Determinism and the Illusion of Freedom

By now you will be able to make sense of the following diagram showing the main possible positions that can be taken on the issue of freedom of action:

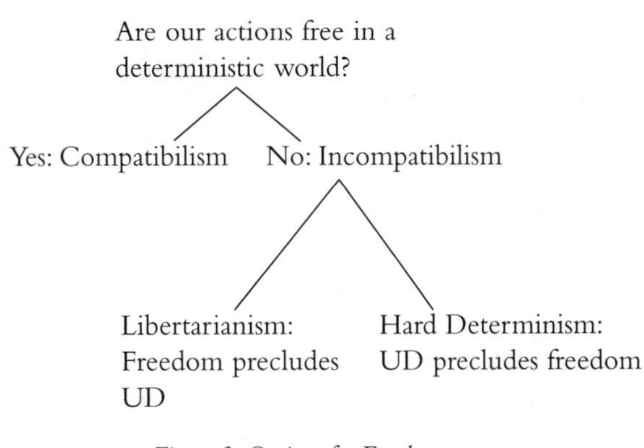

Figure 3: Options for Freedom

Compatibilists such as Hume suggest that universal determinism poses no threat to our having freedom of action. Incompatibilists believe on the other hand that these two phenomena cannot coexist, and so incompatibilists infer that one has got to go. Libertarianism is a form of incompatibilism that infers, from what it takes to be certainty about our free actions, that universal determinism is not true. By contrast, the so-called hard determinist infers, from what it takes to be the certainty of universal determinism, that there is no free will. Could a reasonable person really deny that we have free will? So it seems. First of all, please consider that as scientific knowledge increases, many of our commonsense beliefs become challenged and sometimes rejected. Think of what a shock it must have been some hundreds of years ago to be told that our Earth is round rather than flat, or that it moves around the Sun rather than the Sun moving around it. Yet we now take it for granted that the Earth is round and not at all stationary. Again, it was once thought that when a person is in a cranky, irritable mood it is because of an excess of black vapor, called bile, coming out of his liver. English still even has the adjective "bilious" to describe someone who is in such a mood. Yet while the theory of bile was once commonly accepted, so far as I know no educated person now takes it seriously. We don't know all the causes of cranky moods, but we do know that they can be influenced by such things as blood sugar, hormones, chemical dependence, and lithium levels. We can also be pretty confident that black vapor coming out of your liver won't make it onto this list.

Is any of what you take to be commonsense knowledge of the world really immune to such scientific advances? I suggest that it is quite hard to know what, if anything, would definitely make it onto this "immune list." In particular, it is hard to know how we may be sure that freedom of action will make it onto that list. Perhaps the idea that we perform our actions freely is a holdover from a prescientific age, an idea that in time we will throw onto the trash heap of discarded mythologies along with bile and the geocentric theory of the Earth's place in the cosmos. This at least is what the hard determinist would say. More precisely, the hard determinist, assuming incompatibilism, will infer from what she takes to be the certain truth of universal determinism, the conclusion that freedom of action is an illusion. She might go on to say that she understands that belief in freedom of action is an incredibly appealing and comfortable view. In addition, she might also tell us that she is *not* advocating that we should tell everyone in the world to give up his or her belief in freedom of action. Mythologies, after all, have their place in life.

Well, you might say, if freedom of action is an illusion, then it is also an illusion that, in a given case in which I cause some effect, I could have done otherwise. But if that is right, then it seems awfully hard to know how we can *blame* a person for causing harm, or *praise* a person for producing some good result. Moral praise and blame seem out of place in a world lacking freedom of action. Must the hard determinist, in denying the reality of freedom of action, also deny the very basis of morality, the possibility of praise and blame?

This is a subtle issue, and a topic of current research in philosophy. I'll limit myself to one point here. If you consider some of the ethical theories discussed in Chapter 4, it will be not entirely clear that all such theories presuppose the reality of freedom of will. For instance, the utilitarian theory—according to which that act is right which, from among the alternatives, is most likely to produce the greatest amount of overall happiness—does not, strictly speaking, assume that there are any free actions. In fact, from the point of view of the utilitarian theorist, a robot can perform a morally right action so long as it performs that act which, from among the alternatives, etc. Given this, the utilitarian might say that moral praise and blame have to do, or should have to do, with whether or not an act conforms with its own theory, not with some mythological capacity "to do otherwise." It seems, then, that at least some hard determinists can make sense of the possibility of praise and blame. Whether all hard determinists can do this depends upon what ethical theory they espouse, and settling this question requires in-depth exploration of that ethical theory—not an enterprise for which we have room in this chapter.

Is Conscious Will an Illusion?

If you were impressed with the libertarian's idea that introspection gives us indubitable knowledge of our freedom, you probably also felt suspicious of the hard determinist's conjecture that freedom of action is a current mythology that we will discard with the progress of science. How, you might wonder, will any scientific advance make me give up my introspective certainty? One might as well try to imagine a scientific theory telling me that, contrary to what I think, my tooth really doesn't hurt! If the theory tries to tell me that as I feel the thing throbbing, then so much the worse for the theory!

If only matters were that simple. In fact, we now have pretty striking evidence challenging some of our introspective certainty that our choices cause our behavior. Here is an example: We know in general that a distinctive set of events in the brain occur approximately one second before the onset of a bodily action, even for something so simple as wiggling a finger. In a 1985 study, Libet and colleagues kept this fact in mind while asking subjects to keep their eyes firmly fixed on a large clock in front of them, and the experimenters directed the subjects to make a mental note of when they began consciously to will a finger movement. At the same time, the experimenters gathered information about neural activity in these subjects' brains. That information determined with a good deal of accuracy when the neural events that result in bodily movements, such as raising a finger, began. Accordingly, the researchers were able to compare the times at which the sequence of neural events occur that eventually result in action with the time of occurrence of an agent's experience of consciously willing that action. Amazingly, the neural events often precede the time of consciously willing by a gap of 350–400 milliseconds!

This finding suggests that conscious will is a bit like the steam coming out of a steam engine as it rumbles down the track: The steam is produced by the engine, but doesn't make the engine move. Nevertheless, if the steam were conscious, it would probably take all the credit. Similarly, your conscience experience of willing the action appears to be more a result of an already-begun cascade of neural events, and less a cause of your finger movement. Perhaps I can be sure that I am consciously willing my finger to move, but I may well be wrong in thinking that this conscious will is really doing any causal work.

Wegner and Wheatley draw on Libet's work to put these points in a larger perspective. They argue that people can be brought to have an experience of consciously willing an action in the absence of a causal connection between their will and that action so long as they are convinced (rightly or wrongly) that their conscious willing *precedes,* is *consistent* with, and is an *exclusive* candidate to explain the origin of that action. Consider another study, which is strikingly similar to Taylor's thought experiment (which we discussed earlier in this chapter) involving the neuroscientist who sends radio signals stimulating your brain. Brasil-Neto, et al., magnetically stimulated the motor area of the brain while subjects chose, or tried to choose, to move their right or left index finger. This stimulation produced a strong tendency in subjects to move their finger contralateral to (on the opposite side from) the hemisphere stimulated. Hence if the left hemisphere was magnetically stimulated, subjects would feel a strong urge to move the finger on the right hand. Nevertheless, with or without this stimulation subjects reported feeling fully responsible for the movement of whichever finger moved. Because they were unaware of this stimulation, subjects experienced priority, consistency, and exclusivity and inferred that their conscious will is what moved the finger.

None of these experiments shows that conscious will is *always* an illusion. They do show, however, that our certainty of being the cause of our actions is fallible. In any given case in which you *feel* sure that your conscious will is what makes you act, that feeling might be incorrect. Because of this, trying to undermine UD in the manner of the libertarian is pretty questionable business. After all, we described the libertarian as responding to the problem raised by UD with the observation that since she can be certain that her decisions cause her actions, she can also be sure that UD is not true. Now, however, in light of recent advances in neuroscience we may see that the libertarian has no right to reject UD with such confidence. Perhaps what she thinks is her efficacious conscious will is just a dogma borne of a sense of priority, consistency, and exclusivity.

In each of the last three chapters we raised questions in metaphysics while paying some attention to scientific advances that might help us find, or at least refine, answers. We have little reason to think that scientific theories alone will solve any major philosophical questions. However, one of the most exciting and daunting aspects of recent research in philosophy, psychology, and neuroscience is that findings in each field are of potential interest to findings in the others. This fact is daunting because it is no longer the case that someone concerned with one field can justify completely ignoring the others. On the other hand, it is exciting because it raises the possibility of so many different people learning from one another.

Freedom of Will

We remarked at the beginning of this chapter that freedom of action is different from freedom of will. While freedom of action is a matter of freely performing one action rather than another, freedom of will is a matter of having freedom over your will; that is, freedom over what kind of desires motivate you to act. My liking of cake motivates me to eat more of it than I should, and I would like to change that desire, if only to weaken it. Having freedom of will requires being able to change one or another aspect of my will and thus requires the power to have the will that I want to have.

A normal person does not have power over every aspect of her will: She can't do much to squelch her desire for nourishment, and it would be by no means easy to overcome her desire for social contact with others. She probably won't want to modify these aspects of her will anyway. Nevertheless, we do sometimes find aspects of our will that we want to change, and part of becoming the person that you want to be may involve making such changes as these. In fact, the contemporary philosopher Harry Frankfurt has gone so far as to claim that a necessary condition of being a person is the possession of freedom of will. On his view, those who either are incapable of guiding their will or take no interest in the possibility of doing so are not persons at all but what he would call "wantons." This certainly goes hand in hand with Shakespeare's remark that,

> Like flies to wanton boys are we to the gods;
> They kill us for their sport. (Shakespeare, *King Lear*)

We need not get sidetracked on the question whether Frankfurt is right to set out this standard for persons; we will revisit the issue in the next chapter. What we may observe at this point is that it is surely true that an important step toward leading a satisfying life is choosing the will that you would like to have, within the constraints of what is feasible. Suppose you would like to want to help others less fortunate than yourself, but at this point you don't have much desire to help them. You might be able to acquire a desire to help others, and thereby effect a change in your will. How might you do that? One way is to spend some time helping others less fortunate and seeing how it feels: You help build a home, contribute to a food drive, teach an adult how to read, or something of the kind. You might do one of these things, like the way it feels, and find yourself wanting to do so again. You're now "acquiring a taste" for helping others less fortunate than you, and you are on the way to changing your will. More generally, trying something new is not just a way of gaining a novel experience; it is also a step on the path toward modifying your will and thereby changing yourself.

It takes self-awareness and maturity not only to stand back from yourself and find out what your will is like but also to undertake to change it. This might be a painstaking process taking years, yet the rewards can be considerable. You might change some of your desires that you don't like but have difficulty resisting. In addition, you might cultivate in yourself traits that you find admirable in others, be they real people or fictional characters. In either case you exercise a freedom that seems to distinguish the human condition from that of any other form of life on our planet. At the same time, however, this *self-sculpting* certainly seems to require knowing what a self is, the topic of our next and final chapter.

Study Questions

1. Please explain the difference between *freedom of action* and *freedom of will*.

2. Explain the concept of universal determinism. In light of this explanation show why it might be thought that if universal determinism is true then there are no free actions.

3. Explain, with the aid of at least one example, why it is often held that freedom of the will is a precondition of moral assessment of action.

4. Our best evidence from physics seems to suggest that the universe is not entirely deterministic. For instance, whether a radioactive atom decays at one moment rather than another seems fundamentally a matter of chance. This seems to show that universal determinism is at best an approximation to the truth. Does the failure of universal determinism neutralize the problem of free will? Please explain your answer.

5. Explain the libertarian's position about free will. On what basis might the libertarian hold that by introspecting on your own deliberation, particularly in situations of moral struggle, you can discern that universal determinism is not true?

6. Does the hard determinist's claim that free will is an illusion imply that morality is an illusion as well? Please explain your answer.

7. David Hume defends what is known as compatibilism. Explain in general the compatibilist's position, and show how Hume offers an analysis of what it is for a person to be free (to have what Hume calls "liberty") in terms of a conditional statement. Why would Hume claim that if his analysis of freedom is correct then free will is compatible with universal determinism?

8. Richard Taylor argues that Hume's "conditional" analysis of freedom is incorrect. How would Taylor use his example of the ingenious physiologist to object to Hume's analysis? In your answer be sure to explain how Taylor tries to show that there is a difference in meaning between "x could have done otherwise" and "had x chosen to do otherwise, x would have done."

9. Recent research in neuroscience suggests that we can be tricked into thinking that our consciously willing an action causes that action to occur. Please explain how the research suggests this.

10. Please explain how the phenomenon of freedom of will suggests that within certain limits self-sculpting might be possible.

Suggestions for Further Reading

Pereboom, Derk, ed. *Free Will.* Indianapolis: Hackett Publishing Company, 1997.

Laplace, Pierre Simon. *Philosophical Essay on Probabilities.* Translated from the 5th French edition of 1825 by A. Dale. New York: Springer-Verlag, 1995.

Hume, David. *A Treatise of Human Nature.* 1739. Edited by P. H. Nidditch. Oxford: Oxford University Press, 1978.

Loux, M. *Metaphysics: A Contemporary Introduction.* London: Routledge, 1998.

Taylor, R. *Metaphysics.* Upper Saddle River, NJ: Prentice-Hall, 1963.

Libet, B. "Unconscious Cerebral Initiative and the Role of Conscious Will in Voluntary Action." *Behavioral and Brain Sciences* 8 (1985), pp. 529–66.

Brasil-Neto, J. P., Pascaul-Leone, A., Valls-Solé, J., Cohen, L. G., and Hallett, M. "Focal Transcranial Magnetic Stimulation and Response Bias in a Forced-choice Task." *Journal of Neurology, Neurosurgery, and Psychiatry* 55 (1992), pp. 964–66.

Wegner, D., and T. Wheatley. "Apparent Mental Causation: Sources of the Experience of Will." *American Psychologist* 54 (1999), pp. 480–92.

Wegner, D. *The Illusion of Conscious Will.* Cambridge, MA: MIT Press, 2002.

Frankfurt, H. "Freedom of Will and the Concept of a Person." Reprinted in *Free Will.* Edited by G. Watson. 2nd edition. New York: Oxford, 2003.

Movies Significant for Freedom of Will

The Manchurian Candidate (1962), directed by John Frankenheimer.

Gattaca (1997), directed by Andrew Niccol.

7. What Is a Person?

In the fall of 2004, anthropologists working on the Indonesian island of Flores discovered skeletal remains of a three-foot-tall, flat-faced, bipedal hominid that had inhabited the area as recently as 12,000 years ago. This hominid was strikingly different from other well-known species such as *Homo habilis* and *Homo erectus,* and it has been named *Homo floresiensis. Floresiensis'* skeletal remains were found in caves, together with stone tools of some intricacy as well as evidence of fire-making and of the hunting of large game. This discovery sparked a lively debate in the press and popular scientific publications concerning the status of these creatures. For instance, the popular science writer Desmond Morris asked, if we were to come upon a tribe of these creatures living today, should we treat them as advanced apes or as a form of human being?[1]

Morris raises a good question, but his question is a bit out of focus. The category "human being" is a biological one, and *Homo erectus, Homo sapiens,* and *Homo floresiensis* all belong in it. However, we cannot simply assume that being a *human being* and being a *person* are the same thing. In fact, being a person is the crucial issue. If *Homo floresiensis* is a person, then if we were to encounter one now we would be encountering a creature that has a moral status different in kind from a cat or a horse. For instance, while killing a cat might be morally wrong it is not murder; by contrast, if *floresiensis* is a person, then killing it certainly is.

Perhaps one can be a human being without being a person. If you suffer a terrible accident resulting in such grave brain damage that you enter an irretrievably vegetative state, then perhaps you cease to be a person while remaining a human being. Others hold that infants are human beings but not (yet) persons. It may also be possible to be a person without being a human being. From our discussion of Chapter 5, you can easily imagine why one might hold that a sufficiently sophisticated computer could be a person without being a human being. Or again, one can imagine encountering a race of advanced aliens who, in spite of not being biologically like us at all, are persons but not human beings.

[1] "Eton or the Zoo," from the *BBC World Service,* Friday, October 29, 2004.

Since we cannot just assume that, like a human being, being a person is a biological category, it does not seem that we can settle what a person is by looking through a microscope or excavating a prehistoric hearth. So how might we go about settling the question, what counts as a person? A first suggestion might be to settle it by our decision how to use the word "person." If you reflect on this suggestion, however, it may not seem right. Imagine that country K takes over the world and decrees that heretofore all human beings with an IQ less than 100 are not persons. Country K might even enforce this rule with the result that those of less than average IQ come to be used for invasive experiments and as forced organ donors for the rest of society. Any dissenters to this policy, no matter their IQ, are liquidated. As a result, the new society stipulates that "person" shall be used only to refer to those with above-average IQ, and, of course, after some time everyone is using the word accordingly.

In spite of the new stipulation, however, this does not seem to be a case in which a change has been made in what it is to *be* a person. For instance, some inhabitants of country K might (secretly) feel that their rulers have made an unjust decree. They might feel that their rulers are mistaken in treating these less intelligent human beings as nonpersons. It certainly doesn't seem that we can prove these skeptics wrong by claiming that being a person is a matter of convention. Again, in many societies it is only within the last few centuries that women have come to be viewed as persons rather than as property of their husbands. If you were to travel through time and visit one of the societies in which women were treated as property rather than persons, you would probably feel that the society is (among other things) mistaken in treating women as nonpersons, in spite of that society's conventions. If you take that view, though, you are in effect denying that being a person is a matter of convention. So how else might we make progress on what it is to be a person? A first step is to distinguish two different questions that may be asked with the words, 'What is a person?'

Synchronic and Diachronic Questions of Identity

"Synchronic" has to do with how things are at a certain time. In contrast, "diachronic" has to do with how things are over a stretch of time. Accordingly, one thing that may be being asked with the words, "What is a person?" is a synchronic question about what it is for a thing to be a person *at* a particular time. (Can a computer, an infant, a *Homo floresiensis,* etc., be a person?) In contrast, by asking, "What is a person?" we may also be asking what it is for a person to persist *through* time. This latter question is a bit more complicated than the synchronic question. To formulate it more fully, imagine that P_1 is a moment of a person's life. P_1 is evanescent while the person's life may be very long, yet P_1 will contain experiences, thoughts, emotions, and probably also memories. P_1 is what we may call a *person-stage*. Imagine now that P_2 is also a person-stage, and that it occurs later than P_1. In asking the diachronic question of personal identity, we are asking what it is for a later person-stage such as P_2 to belong to the same person as the earlier stage P_1. For instance, in the movie *The Return of Martin Guerre,* a man abandons his young wife and French village and no one hears word of him for many years. After over a decade, an older man returns to both the village and the woman, professing to be the man who left years ago. The older man knows a great deal about the woman and the village, and many people take him for the man who left earlier. In asking the diachronic question of personal identity, we are asking what it is for this later stage to be one and the same person who left the village years ago.

With this clarification in aid of understanding personal identity we will be trying to fill in the ellipses in the following two different questions:

> *The synchronic question of personal identity:* Person-stage P_1 is a person if and only if . . .

> *The diachronic question of personal identity:* Person stage P_1 is a stage of the same person as person-stage P_2 if and only if . . .[2]

For reasons that will emerge later, we will approach the synchronic question first.

[2] Please note that I do not assume that a person is essentially or necessarily a person. One can ask this diachronic question while keeping open the possibility that I can lose my characteristic of being a person just as I could lose the characteristic of being a citizen of the United States.

Synchronic Identity

The case of *Homo floresiensis* might seem a bit esoteric. However, questions about what it takes to be person in the synchronic sense are hotly debated today, and in some cases entire social policies depend on how we answer them. For instance, proponents of the Great Ape Project have mounted a campaign to include the great apes—chimpanzees, gorillas, orangutans, etc.—among the category of persons. On their website one can read a statement of their overarching mission:

> The Great Ape Project is an idea, a book, and an organization. The idea is radical but simple: to include the non-human great apes within the community of equals by granting them the basic moral and legal protection that only human beings currently enjoy. The book, which is the collective work of a group of scientists and scholars, is a multifaceted argument against the unthinking denial of fundamental rights to beings who are not members of our own species, but who quite evidently possess many of the characteristics that we consider morally important. The organization is an international group founded to work for the removal of the non-human great apes from the category of property, and for their immediate inclusion within the category of persons. (http://www.greatapeproject.org)

If we accept the contention of the Great Ape Project we will accept great apes as persons. As we mentioned a moment ago, doing so will require the ascription of certain basic rights to great apes, and this change will almost certainly require modification of current practices. For instance, your great uncle might be pretty bizarre, and he might do things that have to be seen to be believed. If, however, I were to suggest to you that we should put him in a zoo for all to see, you'd probably be offended, and you might reply with a remark such as, "I admit that Uncle Morris is odd, but he's a person, not an animal; you can't put him in a zoo!" That is quite a reasonable thing to say. However, if the contention of the Great Ape Project is correct, then we have no right displaying gorillas, orangutans, and other great apes in zoos either. Similar points apply to torture, experimentation, and destruction of habitat.

If the Great Ape Project is to convince the world of its claims, it will have to explain what morally important characteristics make an entity a person. Presumably the proponents of this movement will not argue that great apes have souls. It is hard to know how they could convince the world of this claim. More plausibly, proponents of this movement might hearken back to Harry Frankfurt's claim, discussed in Chapter 6, that being a person corresponds to having freedom of will as opposed to freedom of action. Those who think that infants and young children are persons will doubt Frankfurt's claim, since it is unlikely that these two groups have freedom of will in his sense. On the other hand, we might distill out of Frankfurt's position the idea that self-consciousness is a sufficient, if perhaps not a necessary, condition for being a person. (We may leave aside the question whether one can use this self-consciousness to effect changes in one's will.) If that is plausible, then we may now note that *great apes do show evidence of a form of self-consciousness*. For example, a chimpanzee shows considerable evidence of understanding that what she sees in a mirror is herself there rather than another chimp. Given a hand mirror, for instance, she will promptly use it to examine two areas that she cannot normally see—the inside of her mouth and her rear end.

Given our remarks about chauvinism in Chapter 5, we might well reflect on whether being a *Homo sapiens* is necessary and sufficient for being a person. Perhaps that biological category is arbitrary if our concern is with persons as moral agents. This, at least, is the contention of the Great Ape Project, and that contention is not one that we can rule out immediately unless we are to be dogmatic. More generally, self-consciousness seems a not unreasonable criterion for synchronic identity. However, as I just indicated, if we set this up as a necessary, rather than just sufficient, condition for being a person, we will have trouble counting infants as persons; likewise, those with severe mental disability. One challenge, then, as you consider the nature of synchronic identity, is to include as many members of our own species as possible who merit that treatment, without ruling out other species arbitrarily. This question will only become more pressing in the years to come as we develop our understanding of species other than ourselves. In the meantime we do well to turn to diachronic questions.

Memory Links and Identity over Time

A natural first thought about how we might answer the question raised by *The Return of Martin Guerre* is this: The man who returns many years later is the same person as the one who left earlier just in case the returning man can *remember* things that happened to the earlier stage. This point requires an immediate clarification. We might seem to remember things that did not in fact happen to us. For instance, my daughter once was convinced that she and I had once seen a bear outside of a doughnut shop, and she talked about the "memory" frequently. However, I'm certain that I've never taken her to a doughnut shop, much less seen a bear outside of one. My guess is that she had a vivid dream in which this bear sighting happened, and then later she mistook it for a memory. These things are not uncommon. Cases of this kind I shall call *apparent memory* to distinguish them from *genuine memory*. This distinction allows us to clarify our earlier hypothesis as follows:

> *Diachronic personal identity theory 1:* Person stage P_1 is a stage of the same person as person-stage P_2 if and only if P_2 can genuinely remember experiences had by P_1.

As it turns out, the later person-stage only *apparently* remembers experiences had by the earlier person-stage of Martin Guerre. The man who returns to the village is an imposter who had befriended the real Martin abroad and learned so much about him that he decided to attempt to stand in for him back in Martin's village. Unfortunately, the real Martin eventually shows up back in the village and unmasks the imposter, who is hanged for his impersonation. That series of events comports with our diachronic theory 1 above, for the imposter who comes to the village only seems to remember experiences had by the earlier person-stage, but does not genuinely remember them.

This theory also makes good sense of John Locke's famous case of the prince and the cobbler.[3] Modifying the case for present purposes, imagine a prince whose brain and other parts of his central nervous system have been transplanted one night into the body of a cobbler; a symmetrical operation has been performed on the cobbler. Here it seems very plausible that the prince wakes up with the body of a cobbler, and the cobbler with the body of the prince. One might explain that fact by noting that the later person-stage of the prince, waking up in the cobbler's bed, can remember experiences had by the earlier person-stage of the prince surrounded by courtesans. Likewise the later person-stage of the cobbler, waking up in the prince's bed, can remember experiences had by the earlier person-stage of the cobbler surrounded by the tools of his humble trade. It seems that both the prince and the cobbler have had "body transplants" while retaining their central nervous systems.

[3] Locke, J. *Essay Concerning Human Understanding,* edited by P. Nidditch. Oxford: Oxford University Press, 1975, p. 30.

This diachronic theory of personal identity over time is due to Locke and is sometimes referred to as a form of *psychological continuity theory*. It is not without its detractors. For instance, the Scottish philosopher Thomas Reid (1710–96), writing a century after Locke, challenged Locke's very reliance on psychological continuity as the deciding factor. Reid first suggests that while psychological continuity might be *evidence* of personal identity over time, it is not what *makes* for such identity over time. Locke, I'm sure, would not be terribly bothered by this challenge and would want some evidence for the claim. Reid gives just this, writing,

> Although memory gives the most irresistible evidence of my being the identical person that did such a thing, at such a time, I may have other good evidence of things which befell me, and which I do not remember: I know who bare me, and who suckled me, but I do not remember these events. (*Essays on the Intellectual Powers of Man,* Cambridge, MA: MIT Press)

I cannot remember being nursed by my mother at age six weeks, though she assures me that I did nurse at this age. Surely, though, I am the same person as the one who was nursed by her those many years ago. Further, even if you doubt that I was a person as an infant, the same point applies to any experiences, at a tender age or not, of which I have no memory for whatever reason.

Reid poses a good challenge to Locke's psychological continuity theory, but that theory has the resources to respond to it, for we may weaken the theory while retaining its spirit. Perhaps I cannot remember things that befell me when I was a young child. However, I can remember things that befell earlier person-stages, who could remember things that befell earlier person-stages, who could remember things that befell . . . all the way back to experiences had by the young child. Thus whereas Locke's original diachronic personal identity theory 1 suggests a picture like this:

Figure 4: An Illustration of Diachronic Personal Identity Theory 1

A revised version of that theory would suggest a picture like the following:

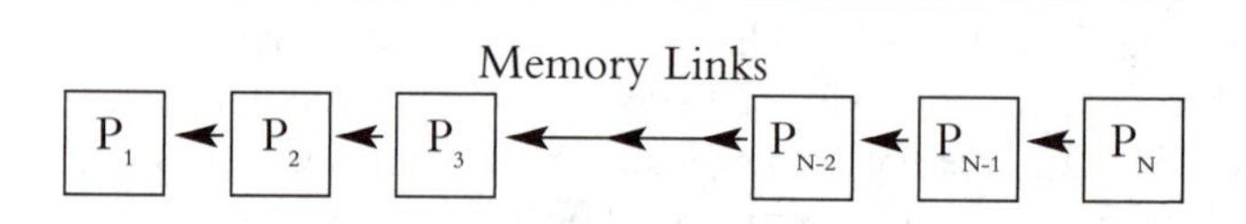

Figure 5: An Illustration of Diachronic Personal Identity Theory 2

where, as in Figure 4, all the arrows represent memory links. Here, so long as there are a finite number of person-stages between P_N and P_1, each of which can remember the preceding person-stage, then P_N and P_1 are stages of the same person. Further, you can slice things as finely as you like, so that two adjacent person-stages are only a few moments apart from one another.

A little reflection shows that this modification is required to save Locke's theory from inconsistency even leaving aside Reid's objection. For imagine an old general (OG) who recalls his bravery on the battlefield as a young captain (YC). The young captain in turn remembers stealing apples from a neighbor's tree as a little boy (LB).[4] According to Locke's theory, OG is one and the same person as YC, and YC is one and the same person as LB. Further, identity generally, and personal identity specifically, seem to be transitive; that is, if A is the same person as B, and B is the same person as C, then A is the same person as C. Hence it just follows on Locke's theory that OG is the same person as LB. His original theory denies this (since OG does not remember experiences had by LB). Hence it requires a modification such as the following:

> *Diachronic personal identity theory 2:* Person-stage P_1 is a stage of the same person as person-stage P_N (where N is finite) if and only if P_N can genuinely remember experiences had by person-stage P_{N-1}, which can remember experiences had by person-stage P_{N-2}, which can remember. . . which can remember experiences had by person-stage P_1.

Figure 5 above illustrates this theory, which accounts for the old general case, as well as permitting Locke a cogent reply to Reid. However, we are not yet out of the woods. For although diachronic personal

[4] This example is drawn from J. Perry, "Introduction," in Perry, ed., *Personal Identity.* Berkeley: University of California Press, p. 17.

identity theory 2 improves upon the earlier theory it is still not adequate. First of all, consider Lenny from the movie, *Memento*. Lenny has had an accident resulting in a severe form of amnesia known as anterograde amnesia. Although he can recall things from before the accident, he literally can't make new memories. In one chase scene in the movie, for instance, he can't even remember whether he is chasing the other guy or the other guy is chasing him! In spite of having tattooed various statements onto his skin, he cannot be sure whether the person-stage that tattooed those statements had his facts straight. Consider two person-stages of Lenny existing after the accident. Because of the severity of his amnesia, these two stages cannot be connected along the lines of diachronic personal identity theory 2. Yet it seems clear that they are two stages of the same person. Can you think of a way of changing the letter while retaining the spirit of diachronic personal identity theory 2, in order to deal with the puzzling case of Lenny?

Bodily Continuity and Identity over Time

We have seen a diachronic personal identity theory in terms of psychological continuity prove its mettle against some hard cases. However, there are reasons for doubting any theory of personal identity over time that appeals to psychological continuity as a criterion. Consider yet another case. Imagine a machine, the duplicator machine, which could make a molecule-for-molecule duplicate of you, including everything in your central nervous system, where, presumably, your memories are stored. If that duplicate of you were created, it would at least *appear* to remember things that happened earlier in your life: It can describe in detail your seventh birthday party, your high school graduation, what you had for lunch yesterday, and so forth. You are now faced with the prospect of entering the duplicator machine. There's one small issue I forgot to mention: After the duplication process is complete, the body that entered the machine will be destroyed in order to prevent confusion among your family, friends, employers, and so forth. The question is now: Even if you are certain that the duplicator machine will make a perfectly accurate copy of your body, would you enter it?

I don't think I would. Perhaps I'm just being timorous, but my sense is that if I were to enter that machine, a copy of me would be made, I would then be destroyed, and then some other being just like me would come into existence. (With luck he will take over my roles in life so that I won't be missed!) If you were considering entering that machine, wouldn't you, too, feel that among other things you were about to be killed? If you do feel this way, then that is reason for doubting any version of the psychological continuity theory.

Perhaps, then, Thomas Reid was right in suggesting that psychological continuity is, at best, evidence of personal identity over time but is not what constitutes it. Yet what other theory might we offer to explain personal identity over time? Some would say that the body is more important to diachronic identity than we have given it credit for thus far. Even in our Locke-inspired example of the prince and the cobbler, we did assume that each person gets to retain his central nervous system. Further, while various neurons in my central nervous system can be replaced one by one over a long period of time, and perhaps also large numbers of them can be replaced at once with a prosthetic device yet to be invented, it is hard to see how I could lose my entire central nervous system in one fell swoop and survive the change. This observation suggests another criterion of diachronic identity:

> *Diachronic personal identity theory 3:* Person-stage P_1 is a stage of the same person as person-stage P_2 if and only if P_1 and P_2 share the same body or same body component such as their central nervous system.

This theory makes good sense of our practices in keeping track of personal identity over time. For instance, to determine whether the suspect in front of us is the person who committed a certain heinous crime a year ago, we will likely resort to fingerprints, and, if possible, DNA evidence to answer this question. Further, even if he cannot recall committing the crime, we might still rely upon physical evidence to show that he is the one who performed it. (His ability to recall the crime seems more relevant to how we punish him if he is found guilty.) That suggests that according at least to forensic science, bodily (as opposed to psychological) continuity is the heart of diachronic identity.

You might challenge diachronic personal identity theory 3 by remarking that many major religious traditions have a well-entrenched conception of disembodied survival after death. Disembodied survival does seem conceivable, even to many who are not theists. Further, if disembodied survival is possible, then bodily continuity is not required for diachronic identity. However, not everything conceivable is really possible. I can conceive of traveling into the past in a time machine, but this does not show that time travel is possible anywhere outside of my imagination. Further, when we suspect that a conceivable situation might not really be possible, we can often confirm that suspicion by revealing a hidden inconsistency in the conceived-of situation. For instance, if time travel were really possible, then I could travel back to the year I was born and strangle the infant Mitchell Green in his crib. But then I would have murdered myself while surviving the event! That doesn't seem possible.

As with the case of time travel, the proponent of the bodily criterion theory of diachronic identity might point out that disembodied existence turns out to be incoherent on closer scrutiny. For instance, if survival after the destruction of the body were really possible, then it should also be possible for not just one, but *two* beings to exist, *both* of whom seem to recall vividly my life here on Earth. Each of these disembodied beings has as good a right to be counted as me as does the other. Which one is me? Are they both me? Then, by transitivity of identity, they are one person also, just inhabiting two different states of consciousness. This seems very strange. On the other hand, if one of them is me, but not the other, what, if anything, could make this the case? In fact, there could be thousands of disembodied beings all of whom are vying for the status of being me. These consequences suggest that the idea of disembodied existence is, at the very least, puzzling. Simply from the conceivability of this event, we cannot infer that it is genuinely possible. Accordingly, the proponent of the bodily continuity theory of diachronic identity might be skeptical that disembodied existence is really possible, and her skepticism would not be without basis. For that reason, we can't refute the bodily continuity theory by invoking claims about life after death.

We also can't refute that theory by pointing out that I persist while any part of my central nervous system can be replaced. This latter claim is certainly true: If a part of my brain, say my amygdala (which apparently is responsible for many of my emotional responses) stops working, we can imagine engineers and doctors someday being in a position to replace it with a prosthetic device. It seems clear that if that were to happen, the person-stage who is the proud owner of the prosthetic amygdala could be the same person as the person-stage who had the deteriorating amygdala in need of replacement. The bodily continuity theory of diachronic identity can take this in stride by remarking that many material objects can persist even while some of their component parts change. Theseus, imagine, had a ship that left for its maiden voyage in the year 100 AD. After returning to port its owners found that a few planks had rotted, and replaced them. Surely the ship with new planks is the same as the one that left on its voyage in 100 AD? If so, then the fact that a material object can survive replacement of some of its parts is no skin off the back of the bodily continuity theory of diachronic personal identity.

While deep challenges face any form of psychological continuity theory of diachronic identity, the bodily continuity theory seems hard to swallow even after the above clarifications. Not many people can resist the sentiment that we could survive the destruction of our bodies, including our central nervous systems. It is the same sentiment that enabled Descartes to argue for his dualism in Chapter 5 on the basis of the possibility of surviving the death of one's body. In fact, it is the same sentiment that enabled Socrates to drink hemlock with equanimity after being sentenced to death by his fellow Athenians for allegedly corrupting the youth of the city. If diachronic identity consists in bodily continuity, however, this sentiment is illusory. Could that really be? If it is, then philosophy teaches us that some of our most heartfelt convictions need to be given up.

In the Introduction to this book I suggested that being alive to a single philosophical question seems to require keeping an eye on many others at once: Questions about the existence of God connect with questions of ethics, of what it is to be a person, of what it means to be free; questions, as we have just seen, of freedom connect not just with those of God's existence but also of what it means to be conscious as well as with questions of neuroscience and physics. A pessimist might conclude that this shows philosophy to be impossible, since one can only solve one problem by solving all the others first. However, that conclusion would be rash. Another response to this situation is to see philosophy as a field that never sleeps: Answering our pressing questions requires all of our vigilance, sensitivity, and imagination. This can be daunting. On the other hand, it can enrich your life by making you alive to connections that may have eluded your attention thus far. If that happens, then you've begun engaging philosophy.

Study Questions

1. Please explain the difference between diachronic and synchronic questions of personal identity. What is John Locke's original, unrefined view of diachronic personal identity? In light of this position, explain why Locke holds that a person can survive the loss of her body, and even the loss of her brain? Next, show how Locke attempts to bolster his thesis by means of his example of the prince and the cobbler.

2. Is Locke's theory of diachronic personal identity compatible with the possibility of more than one person inhabiting a single body, as appears to be the case with clinical examples of multiple personality? Please explain your answer.

3. Thomas Reid denies that diachronic personal identity requires continuity of memory. After explaining the Old General Paradox, show how it is a challenge to Locke's unrefined theory of diachronic personal identity. Could Locke refine this theory of diachronic personal identity in order to accommodate the Old General Paradox? Please explain your answer.

4. How might the example of *Memento*'s Lenny, who suffers from anterograde amnesia, challenge even Locke's refined theory of diachronic personal identity?

5. Why might it be thought that any theory of diachronic personal identity founders on the possibility "fission," in which one person's memories seem to be transferred into two different bodies?

6. Assuming that you have no desire to commit suicide, would you step into a "duplicator machine" as described in this chapter? Please explain your answer.

7. How might one defend a conception of diachronic personal identity in terms of bodily continuity?

8. Does the bodily continuity theory leave open the possibility of surviving the total destruction of your body?

9. Suppose a defender of the Great Ape Project tries to argue that, for instance, chimpanzees should be counted as persons just as much as human beings should. How might she defend that conclusion? Might empirical research be relevant to supporting or rebutting her contention? Please explain your answer.

10. Please explain what it might mean to modify one's own will. Might the ability to modify one's own will be pertinent to the issue of being a person in the synchronic sense? Please explain your answer. Might the ability to modify one's own will be pertinent to the issue of having free will? Please explain your answer.

Suggestions for Further Reading

Locke, John. *Essay Concerning Human Understanding.* Edited by P. Nidditch. Oxford: Oxford University Press, 1975.

Perry, J. *Personal Identity.* Berkeley: University of California Press, 1978.

Perry, J. *Identity, Personal Identity, and the Self.* Indianapolis: Hackett Publishing Company, 2002.

Perry, J. *A Dialogue on Personal Identity and Immortality.* Indianapolis: Hackett Publishing Company, 1978.

Movies Significant for Personal Identity

The Return of Martin Guerre (1982), directed by Daniel Vigne.

Memento (2000), directed by Chris Nolan.

Fight Club (1999), directed by David Fincher.

Philosophical Glossary

agnostic: A person who neither believes in the existence of God (defined as the Greatest Conceivable Being), nor believes that God does not exist.

a priori: Knowledge that can be attained without the aid of empirical inquiry. An example is the Pythagorean theorem: We know this to be true without having to do experiments or surveys. Hume's characters in the *Dialogues* differ over whether God's existence can be proven by a priori means.

a posteriori: Knowledge that can be attained only with the aid of empirical investigation. Most of physical, life, and social science is aimed at the attainment of a posteriori knowledge.

argument: A line of reasoning purporting to establish a conclusion. An argument comprises one or more premises; possibly, but not necessarily, intermediate steps; and a conclusion.

atheist: A person who believes that God (defined as the Greatest Conceivable Being) does not exist.

compatibilism: The doctrine that freedom of action and universal determinism are compatible with one another.

conclusion: The statement that an argument is attempting to establish.

defense: A line of reasoning purporting to show that the existence of some evil, either moral or physical, is compatible with the existence of a GCB.

dependent being: An entity that has the cause of its existence in something other than itself. (Everyday objects, such as tables, rocks, and clouds are dependent beings.)

dualism: The doctrine that the world consists of two kinds of substance, neither reducible to the other. Typically, dualists hold that mind and matter constitute the distinct kinds of substance in question.

epistemology: The philosophical study of the nature and scope of knowledge.

ethical egoism: The doctrine that what makes an act right is its being the one that either is, or is most likely to, produce the overall greatest amount of happiness for me.

fallacy: An unpersuasive argument. Some arguments are fallacies because they are invalid. Others, such as arguments that beg the question, are unpersuasive because they give us no reason to accept the conclusion.

functionalism: A doctrine concerning the nature of mental states, holding that what makes something a mental state of a particular type does not depend on its internal constitution, but instead on the role it plays, in conjunction with other mental states, in the system of which it is a part.

God: The being who has all possible perfections. This means that for any characteristic C, if C is a perfection, then God has characteristic C. (This definition does not assume that such a being exists.) We refer to God so defined as the GCB (Greatest Conceivable Being).

Hard determinism: A form of incompatibilism holding that universal determinism implies that no actions are free.

Hume's principle: Once you've explained the features of each element in a totality, you have explained the features of the totality as well.

identity of indiscernibles: If a and b have all the same properties, then they are identical. (This thesis is *not* used by Descartes in his argument for the distinctness of mind and body.)

incompatibilism: The doctrine that freedom of action and universal determinism are not compatible with one another.

independent being: An entity that has the cause of its existence in itself. (Many philosophers, such as Samuel Clarke, have taken God to be an independent being.)

indiscernibility of identicals: If entities a and b are identical, then they have all the same properties.

infinite causal regression: A series of causes stretching back in time infinitely, so that for each element e_n in the series there is some prior event e_{n-1} that caused e_n.

invalid argument: An argument is invalid just in case it is not valid.

libertarianism: A form of incompatibilism holding that the existence of free will proves that universal determinism is not true. Libertarians sometimes hold that free will can be established just by introspection.

materialism: A form of monism holding that all existing things are either made of or are reducible to matter.

monism: The doctrine that the universe consists of just one kind of stuff. This view may take the form either of materialism (all that there is is made of or is reducible to matter), or idealism (all that there is is made of or reducible to mind).

moral evil: The production of a harm or suffering by a free agent who acts while aware of the harmful consequences of his/her act. The existence of moral evil has traditionally raised doubts for some about God's alleged omnibenevolence, omnipotence, and omniscience.

natural religion: The attempt to establish the existence of God by means of theoretical rationality. Hume in his *Dialogues* is concerned primarily with natural religion, though his character Demea is doubtful that such an attempt can succeed.

ontology: The study of what there is. Consequently, the ontological argument is an attempt to prove the *existence* of God.

physical evil: The production of a harm or suffering by something other than a free, knowing agent. An innocent infant's death by SIDS (sudden infant death syndrome) is an example of physical evil, since it is a harm that is not brought about by any free agent's action. The existence of physical evil has traditionally raised doubts for some about God's alleged omnibenevolence, omnipotence, and omniscience.

possible world: A state of affairs that might have been. Strictly speaking, the actual world, the actual state of affairs, is also a possible world.

practical rationality: An act is practically rational just in case it is most likely to best serve one's interests, given the relative ranking of those interests and the likely outcomes of the actions available. (A special case of such acts is the formation of a belief.)

premise: A statement used as a starting point in an argument. Normally, premises should be uncontroversial theses that most people would assent to. However, sometimes one may criticize an argument by challenging one or more of its premises.

principle of sufficient reason: The doctrine that every fact or state of affairs has a reason that explains its truth or existence. The principle of sufficient reason has broader scope than the doctrine of universal determinism.

quotidian moral relativism: An empirical claim, familiar from cultural anthropology, that we find a considerable variety of opinions on questions of right and wrong throughout space and time.

reductio ad absurdum: A line of reasoning showing that a certain proposition is false. It does this by showing that assuming (for the sake of argument) that this proposition is true implies something that we know to be false. We can, for instance, "reduce to absurdity" the supposition that there is a largest integer.

revealed religion: An approach to religion that takes God's existence for granted and attempts a union with God or to come to understand God's attributes.

robust moral relativism: There is no perspective-independent fact of the matter as to what is right or wrong; rather the only facts about morality that exist are relative to a point of view. (This point of view might be constituted by a society, a culture, an ethnicity, or even an individual, and different forms of robust relativism will flow from different ways of understanding what sorts of entities moral facts are relative to.)

theist: Someone who believes in the existence of God (defined as the Greatest Conceivable Being).

theodicy: A line of reasoning purporting to show that the amount of moral and physical evil that actually exists in the world is compatible with God's being the GCB. A theodicy goes beyond a defense.

theoretical rationality: A belief is theoretically rational just in case it is reasonable to hold it given all the evidence available.

Turing test: A criterion proposed by Alan Turing for determining whether it is possible for a machine to think. The test consists of putting a computer in a closed room and interrogating it with typed questions. Turing proposes that if, on the basis of this examination, the interrogator cannot determine whether what is in the room is a machine or a person, then it follows that the machine can think.

universal determinism: Every material event has a prior sufficient material condition.

utilitarianism: An ethical doctrine telling us to perform that act, from those available, most likely to produce the greatest overall amount of happiness.

Index